Architecture and Democracy

Claude Fayette Bragdon

PREFACE

This book can lay no claim to unity of theme, since its subjects range from skyscrapers to symbols and soul states; but the author claims for it nevertheless a unity of point of view, and one (correct or not) so comprehensive as to include in one synthesis every subject dealt with. For according to that point of view, a skyscraper is only a symbol—and of what? A condition of consciousness, that is, a state of the soul. Democracy even, we are beginning to discover, is a condition of consciousness too.

Our only hope of understanding the welter of life in which we are immersed, as in a swift and muddy river, is in ascending as near to its pure source as we can. That source is in consciousness and consciousness is in ourselves. This is the point of view from which each problem dealt with has been attacked; but lest the author be at once set down as an impracticable dreamer, dwelling aloof in an ivory tower, the reader should know that his book has been written in the scant intervals afforded by the practice of the profession of architecture, so broadened as to include the study of abstract form, the creation of ornament, experiments with color and light, and such occasional educational activities as from time to time he has been called upon to perform at one or another architectural school.

The three essays included under the general heading of "Democracy and Architecture" were prepared at the request of the editor of The Architectural Record, and were published in that journal. The two following, on "Ornament from Mathematics," represent a recasting and a rewriting of articles which have appeared in The Architectural Review, The Architectural Forum, and The American Architect. "Harnessing the Rainbow" is an address delivered before the Ad. Club of Cleveland, and the Rochester Rotary Club, and afterwards made into an essay and published in The American Architect under a different title. The appreciation of Louis Sullivan as a writer appears here for the first time, the author having previously paid his respects to Mr. Sullivan's strictly architectural genius in an essay in House and Garden. "Color and Ceramics" was delivered on the occasion of the dedication of the Ceramic Building of the University of Illinois, and afterwards published in The Architectural Forum. "Symbols and Sacraments" was printed in the English Quarterly Orpheus. "Self Education" was delivered before the Boston Architectural Club, and afterwards published in a number of architectural journals.

Acknowledgment is hereby tendered by the author to the editors of these various magazines for their consent to republication, together with thanks, however belated, for their unfailing hospitality to the children of his brain.

CLAUDE BRAGDON.
August 1, 1918.

CONTENTS

ARCHITECTURE AND DEMOCRACY

I. Before the War

II. During the War

III. After the War

ORNAMENT FROM MATHEMATICS

I. The World Order

II. The Fourth Dimension

HARNESSING THE RAINBOW

LOUIS SULLIVAN, PROPHET OF DEMOCRACY

COLOR AND CERAMICS

SYMBOLS AND SACRAMENTS

SELF-EDUCATION

Every form of government, every social institution, every undertaking, however great, however small, every symbol of enlightenment or degradation, each and all have sprung and are still springing from the life of the people, and have ever formed and are now as surely forming images of their thought. Slowly by centuries, generations, years, days, hours, the thought of the people has changed; so with precision have their acts responsively changed; thus thoughts and acts have flowed and are flowing ever onward, unceasingly onward, involved within the impelling power of Life. Throughout this stream of human life, and thought, and activity, men have ever felt the need to build; and from the need arose the power to build. So, as they thought, they built; for, strange as it may seem, they could build in no other way. As they built, they made, used, and left behind them records of their thinking. Then, as through the years new men came with changed thoughts, so arose new buildings in consonance with the change of thought—the building always the expression of the thinking. Whatever the character of the thinking, just so was the character of the building.

What is Architecture? A Study in the American People of Today, by

LOUIS SULLIVAN.

Architecture and Democracy

I

BEFORE THE WAR

The world war represents not the triumph, but the birth of democracy. The true ideal of democracy—the rule of a people by the *demos*, or group soul—is a thing unrealized. How then is it possible to consider or discuss an architecture of democracy—the shadow of a shade? It is not possible to do so with any degree of finality, but by an intention of consciousness upon this juxtaposition of ideas—architecture and democracy—signs of the times may yield new meanings, relations may emerge between things apparently unrelated, and the future, always existent in every present moment, may be evoked by that strange magic which resides in the human mind.

Architecture, at its worst as at its best, reflects always a true image of the thing that produced it; a building is revealing even though it is false, just as the face of a liar tells the thing his words endeavor to conceal. This being so, let us make such architecture as is ours declare to us our true estate.

The architecture of the United States, from the period of the Civil War, up to the beginning of the present crisis, everywhere reflects a struggle to be free of a vicious and depraved form of feudalism, grown strong under the very ægis of democracy. The qualities that made feudalism endeared and enduring; qualities written in beauty on the cathedral cities of mediaeval Europe—faith, worship, loyalty, magnanimity—were either vanished or banished from this pseudo-democratic, aridly scientific feudalism, leaving an inheritance of strife and tyranny—a strife grown mean, a tyranny grown prudent, but full of sinister power the weight of which we have by no means ceased to feel.

Power, strangely mingled with timidity; ingenuity, frequently misdirected; ugliness, the result of a false ideal of beauty—these in general characterize the architecture of our immediate past; an architecture "without ancestry or hope of posterity," an architecture devoid of coherence or conviction; willing to lie, willing to steal. What impression such a city as Chicago or Pittsburgh might have made upon some denizen of those cathedral-crowned feudal cities of the past we do not know. He would certainly have been amazed at its giant energy, and probably revolted at its grimy dreariness. We are wont to pity the mediaeval man for the dirt he lived in, even while smoke greys our sky and dirt permeates the very air we breathe: we think of castles as grim and cathedrals as dim, but they were beautiful and gay with color compared with the grim, dim canyons of our city streets.

Lafcadio Hearn, in *A Conservative*, has sketched for us, with a sympathy truly clairvoyant, the impression made by the cities of the West upon the consciousness of a young Japanese samurai educated under a feudalism not unlike that of the Middle Ages, wherein was worship, reverence, poetry, loyalty—however strangely compounded with the more sinister products of the feudal state.

> Larger than all anticipation the West appeared to him,—a world of giants; and that which depresses even the boldest Occidental who finds himself, without means or friends, alone in a great city, must often have depressed the Oriental exile: that vague uneasiness aroused by the sense of being invisible to hurrying millions; by the ceaseless roar of traffic drowning voices; by monstrosities of architecture without a soul; by the dynamic display of wealth forcing mind and hand, as mere cheap machinery, to the uttermost limits of the possible. Perhaps he saw such cities as Doré saw London: sullen majesty of arched glooms, and granite deeps opening into granite deeps beyond range of vision, and mountains of masonry with seas of labor in turmoil at their base, and monumental spaces displaying the grimness of ordered power slow-gathering through centuries. Of beauty there was nothing to make appeal to him between those endless cliffs of stone which walled out the sunrise and the sunset, the sky and the wind.

The view of our pre-war architecture thus sketchily presented is sure to be sharply challenged in certain quarters, but unfortunately for us all this is no mere matter of opinion, it is a matter of fact. The buildings are there, open to observation; rooted to the spot, they cannot run away. Like criminals "caught with the goods" they stand, self-convicted, dirty with the soot of a thousand chimneys, heavy with the spoils of vanished civilizations; graft and greed stare at us out of their glazed windows—eyes behind which no soul can be discerned. There are doubtless extenuating circumstances; they want to be clean, they want to be honest, these "monsters of the mere market," but they are nevertheless the unconscious victims of evils inherent in our transitional social state.

Let us examine these strange creatures, doomed, it is hoped, to extinction in favor of more intelligent and gracious forms of life. They are big, powerful, "necessitous," and have therefore an impressiveness, even an æsthetic appeal, not to be denied. So subtle and sensitive an old-world consciousness as that of M. Paul Bourget was set vibrating by them like a violin to the concussion of a trip-hammer, and to the following tune:

> The portals of the basements, usually arched as if crushed beneath the weight of the mountains which they support, look like dens of a primitive race, continually receiving and pouring forth a stream of people. You lift your eyes, and you feel that up there behind the perpendicular wall, with its innumerable windows, is a multitude coming and going,—crowding the offices that perforate these cliffs of brick and iron, dizzied with the speed of the elevators. You divine, you feel the hot breath of speculation quivering behind these windows. This it is which has fecundated these thousands of square feet of earth, in order that from them may spring up this appalling growth of business palaces, that hide the sun from you and almost shut out the light of day.

"The simple power of necessity is to a certain degree a principle of beauty," says M. Bourget, and to these structures this order of beauty cannot be denied, but even this is vitiated by a failure to press the advantage home: the ornate façades are notably less impressive than those whose grim and stark geometry is unmitigated by the grave-clothes of dead styles. Instances there are of strivings toward a beauty that is fresh and living, but they are so unsuccessful and infrequent as to be negligible. However impressive these buildings may be by reason of their ordered geometry, their weight and magnitude, and as a manifestation of irrepressible power, they have the unloveliness of things ignoble being the product neither of praise, nor joy, nor worship, but enclosures for the transaction of sharp bargains—gold bringing jinn of our modern Aladdins, who love them not but only use them. That is the reason they are ugly; no one has loved them for themselves alone.

For beauty is ever the very face of love. From the architecture of a true democracy, founded on love and mutual service, beauty would inevitably shine forth; its absence convicts us of a maladjustment in our social and economic life. A skyscraper shouldering itself aloft at the expense of its more humble neighbors, stealing their air and their sunlight, is a symbol, written large against the sky, of the will-to-power of a man or a group of men—of that ruthless and tireless aggression on the part of the cunning and the strong so characteristic of the period which produced the skyscraper. One of our streets made up of buildings of diverse styles and shapes and sizes—like a jaw with some teeth whole, some broken, some rotten, and some gone—is a symbol of our unkempt individualism, now happily becoming curbed and chastened by a common danger, a common devotion.

Some people hold the view that our insensitiveness to formal beauty is no disgrace. Such argue that our accomplishments and our interests are in other fields, where we more than match the accomplishments of older civilizations. They forget that every achievement not registered in terms of beauty has failed of its final and enduring transmutation. It is because the achievements of older civilizations attained to their apotheoses in art that they interest us, and unless we are able to effect a corresponding transmutation we are destined to perish unhonoured on our rubbish heap. That we shall effect it, through knowledge and suffering, is certain, but before attempting the more genial and rewarding task of tracing, in our life and in our architecture, those forces and powers which make for righteousness, for beauty, let us look our failures squarely in the face, and discover if we can why they are failures.

Confining this examination to the particular matter under discussion, the neo-feudal architecture of our city streets, we find it to lack unity, and the reason for this lack of unity dwells in a *divided consciousness*. The tall office building is the product of many forces, or perhaps we should say one force, that of necessity; but its concrete embodiment is the result of two different orders of talent, that of the structural engineer and of the architectural designer. These are usually incarnate in two different individuals, working more or less at cross purposes. It is the business of the engineer to preoccupy himself solely with ideas of efficiency and economy, and over his efficient and economical structure the designer smears a frosting of beauty in the form of architectural style, in the archæological sense. This is a foolish practice, and cannot but result in failure. In the case of a Greek temple or a mediaeval cathedral structure and style were not twain, but one; the structure determined the style, the style expressed the structure; but with us so divorced have the two things become that in a case known to the author, the structural framework of a great office building was determined and fabricated and then architects were invited to "submit designs" for the exterior. This is of course an extreme example and does not represent the usual practice, but it brings sharply to consciousness the well known fact that for these buildings we have substantially one method of construction—that of the vertical strut, and the horizontal "fill"—while in style they appear as Grecian, Roman, Renaissance, Gothic, Modern French and what not, according to the whim of the designer.

With the modern tendency toward specialization, the natural outgrowth of necessity, there is no inherent reason why the bones of a building should not be devised by one man and its fleshly clothing by another, so long as they understand one another, and are in ideal agreement, but there is in general all too little understanding, and a confusion of ideas and aims. To the average structural engineer the architectural designer is a mere milliner in stone, informed in those prevailing architectural fashions of which he himself knows little and cares less. Preoccupied as he is with the building's strength, safety, economy; solving new and staggeringly difficult problems with address and daring, he has scant sympathy with such inconsequent matters as the stylistic purity of a façade, or the profile of a moulding. To the designer, on the other hand, the engineer appears in the light of a subordinate to be used for the promotion of his own ends, or an evil to be endured as an interference with those ends.

As a result of this lack of sympathy and co-ordination, success crowns only those efforts in which, on the one hand, the stylist has been completely subordinated to engineering necessity, as in the case of the East River bridges, where the architect was called upon only to add a final grace to the strictly structural towers; or on the other hand, in which the structure is of the old-fashioned masonry sort, and faced with a familiar problem the architect has found it easy to be frank; as in the case of the Manhattan Storage Warehouse, on 42nd Street, New York, or in the Bryant Park façade on the New York Library. The Woolworth building is a notable example of the complete co-ordination between the structural framework and its envelope, and falls short of ideal success only in the employment of an archaic and alien ornamental language, used, however, let it be said, with a fine understanding of the function of ornament.

For the most part though, there is a difference of intention between the engineer and the designer; they look two ways, and the result of their collaboration is a flat and confused image of the thing that should be, not such as is produced by truly binocular vision. This difference of aim is largely the result of a difference of education. Engineering science of the sort which the use of steel has required is a thing unprecedented; the engineer cannot hark back to the past for help, even if he would. The case is different with the architectural designer; he is taught that all of the best songs have been sung, all of the true words spoken. The Glory that was Greece, and the Grandeur that was Rome, the romantic exuberance of Gothic, and the ordered restraint of Renaissance are so drummed into him during his years of training, and exercise so tyrannical a spell over his imagination that he loses the power of clear and logical thought, and never becomes truly creative. Free of this incubus the engineer has succeeded in being straightforward and sensible, to say the least; subject to it the man with a so-called architectural education is too often tortuous and absurd.

The architect without any training in the essentials of design produces horrors as a matter of course, for the reason that sin is the result of ignorance; the architect trained in the false manner of the current schools becomes a reconstructive archæologist, handicapped by conditions with which he can deal only imperfectly, and imperfectly control. Once in a blue moon a man arises who, with all the advantages inherent in education, pierces through the past to the present, and is able to use his brain as the architects of the past used theirs—to deal simply and directly with his immediate problem.

Such a man is Louis Sullivan, though it must be admitted that not always has he achieved success. That success was so marked, however, in his treatment of the problem of the tall building, and exercised subconsciously such a spell upon the minds even of his critics and detractors, that it resulted in the emancipation of this type of building from an absurd and impossible convention—the practice, common before his time, of piling order upon order, like a house of cards, or by a succession of strongly marked string courses emphasizing the horizontal dimension of a vertical edifice, thus vitiating the finest effect of which such a building is capable.

The problem of the tall building, with which his predecessors dealt always with trepidation and equivocation, Mr. Sullivan approached with confidence and joy. "What," he asked himself, "is the chief characteristic of the tall office building? It is lofty. This loftiness is to the artist-nature its thrilling aspect. It must be tall. The force of altitude must be in it. It must be every inch a proud and soaring thing, rising in sheer exultation that from bottom to top it is a unit without a dissenting line." The Prudential (Guaranty) building in Buffalo represents the finest concrete embodiment of his idea achieved by Mr. Sullivan. It marks his emancipation from what he calls his "masonry" period, during which he tried, like so many other architects before and since, to make a steel-framed structure look as though it were nothing but a masonry wall perforated with openings—openings too many and too great not to endanger its stability. The keen blade of Mr. Sullivan's mind cut through this contradiction, and in the Prudential building he carried out the idea of a *protective casing* so successfully that Montgomery Schuyler said of it, "I know of no steel framed building in which the metallic construction is more palpably felt through the envelope of baked clay."

The present author can speak with all humbleness of the general failure, on the part of the architectural profession, to appreciate the importance of this achievement, for he pleads guilty of day after day having passed the Prudential building, then fresh in the majesty of its soaring lines, and in the wonder of its fire-wrought casing, with eyes and admiration only for the false romanticism of the Erie County Savings Bank, and the empty bombast of the gigantic Ellicott Square. He had not at that period of his life succeeded in living down his architectural training, and as a result the most ignorant layman was in a better position to appraise the relative merits of these three so different incarnations of the building impulse than was he.

Since the Prudential building there have been other tall office buildings, by other hands, truthful in the main, less rigid, less monotonous, more superficially pleasing, yet they somehow fail to impart the feeling of utter sincerity and fresh originality inspired by this building. One feels that here democracy has at last found utterance in beauty; the American spirit speaks, the spirit of the Long Denied. This rude, rectangular bulk is uncompromisingly practical and utilitarian; these rows on rows of windows, regularly spaced, and all of the same size, suggest the equality and monotony of obscure, laborious lives; the upspringing shafts of the vertical piers stand for their hopes and aspirations, and the unobtrusive, delicate ornament which covers the whole with a garment of fresh beauty is like the very texture of their dreams. The building is able to speak thus powerfully to the imagination because its creator is a poet and prophet of democracy. In his own chosen language he declares, as Whitman did in verse, his faith in the people of "these states"—"A Nation announcing itself." Others will doubtless follow who will make a richer music, commensurate with the future's richer life, but such democracy as is ours stands here proclaimed, just as such feudalism as is still ours stands proclaimed in the Erie County Bank just across the way. The massive rough stone walls of this building, its pointed towers and many dormered chateau-like roof unconsciously symbolize the attempt to impose upon the living present a moribund and alien order. Democracy is thus afflicted, and the fact must needs find architectural expression.

In the field of domestic architecture these dramatic contrasts are less evident, less sharply marked. Domestic life varies little from age to age; a cottage is a cottage the world over, and some manorial mansion on the James River, built in Colonial days, remains a fitting habitation (assuming the addition of electric lights and sanitary plumbing) for one of our Captains of Industry, however little an ancient tobacco warehouse would serve him as a place of business. This fact is so well recognized that the finest type of modern country house follows, in general, this or some other equally admirable model, though it is amusing to note the millionaire's preference for a feudal castle, a French chateau, or an Italian villa of the decadence.

The "man of moderate means," so called, provides himself with no difficulty with a comfortable house, undistinguished but unpretentious, which fits him like a glove. There is a piazza towards the street, a bay-window in the living room, a sleeping-porch for the children, and a box of a garage for the flivver in the bit of a back yard.

For the wage earner the housing problem is not so easily nor so successfully solved. He is usually between the devil of the speculative builder and the deep sea of the predatory landlord, each intent upon taking from him the limit that the law allows and giving him as little as possible for his money. Going down the scale of indigence we find an itinerancy amounting almost to homelessness, or houses so abject that they are an insult to the very name of home.

It is an eloquent commentary upon our national attitude toward a most vital matter that in this feverish hustle to produce ships, airplanes, clothing and munitions on a vast scale, the housing of the workers was either overlooked entirely, or received eleventh-hour consideration, and only now, after a year of participation in the war, is it beginning to be adequately and officially dealt with—how efficiently and intelligently remains to be seen. The housing of the soldiers was another matter: that necessity was plain and urgent, and the miracle has been accomplished, but except by indirection it has contributed nothing to the permanent housing problem.

Other aspects of our life which have found architectural expression fall neither in the commercial nor in the domestic category—the great hotels, for example, which partake of the nature of both, and our passenger railway terminals, which partake of the nature of neither. These latter deserve especial consideration in this connection, by reason of their important function. The railway is of the very essence of the modern, even though (with what sublime unreason) Imperial Rome is written large over New York's most magnificent portal.

Think not that in an age of unfaith mankind gives up the building of temples. Temples inevitably arise where the tide of life flows strongest; for there God manifests, in however strange a guise. That tide is nowhere stronger than in the railroad, which is the arterial system of our civilization. All arteries lead to and from the heart, and thus the railroad terminus becomes the beating heart at the center of modern life. It is a true instinct therefore which prompts to the making of the terminal building a very temple, a monument to the conquest of space through the harnessing of the giant horses of electricity and steam. This conquest must be celebrated on a scale commensurate with its importance, and in obedience to this necessity the Pennsylvania station raised its proud head amid the push-cart architecture of that portion of New York in which it stands. It is not therefore open to the criticism often passed upon it, that it is too grand, but it is the wrong kind of grandeur. If there be truth in the contention that the living needs of today cannot be grafted upon the dead stump of any ancient grandeur, the futility of every attempt to accomplish this impossible will somehow, somewhere, reveal itself to the discerning eye. Let us seek out, in this building, the place of this betrayal.

It is not necessarily in the main façade, though this is not a face, but a mask—and a mask can, after its kind, always be made beautiful; it is not in the nobly vaulted corridor, lined with shops—for all we know the arcades of Imperial Rome were similarly lined; nor is it in the splendid vestibule, leading into the magnificent waiting room, in which a subject of the Cæsars would have felt more perfectly at home, perhaps, than do we. But beyond this passenger concourse, where the elevators and stairways descend to the tracks, necessity demanded the construction of a great enclosure, supported only on slender columns and far-flung trusses roofed with glass. Now latticed columns, steel trusses, and wire glass are inventions of the modern world too useful to be dispensed with. Rome could not help the architect here. The mode to which he was inexorably self-committed in the rest of the building demanded massive masonry, cornices, mouldings; a tribute to Cæsar which could be paid everywhere but in this place. The architect's problem then became to reconcile two diametrically different systems. But between the west wall of the ancient Roman baths and the modern skeleton construction of the roof of the human greenhouse there is no attempt at fusion. The slender latticed columns cut unpleasantly through the granite cornices and mouldings; the first century A.D. and the twentieth are here in incongruous juxtaposition—a little thing, easily overlooked, yet how revealing! How reassuring of the fact "God is not mocked!"

The New York Central terminal speaks to the eye in a modern tongue, with however French an accent. Its façade suggests a portal, reminding the beholder that a railway station is in a very literal sense a city gate placed just as appropriately in the center of the municipality as in ancient times it was placed in the circuit of the outer walls.

Neither edifice will stand the acid test of Mr. Sullivan's formula, that a building is an organism and should follow the law of organisms, which decrees that the form must everywhere follow and express the function, the function determining and creating its appropriate form. Here are two eminent examples of "arranged" architecture. Before organic architecture can come into being our inchoate national life must itself become organic. Arranged architecture, of the sort we see everywhere, despite its falsity, is a true expression of the conditions which gave it birth.

The grandeur of Rome, the splendour of Paris—what just and adequate expression do they give of modern American life? Then shall we find in our great hotels, say, such expression? Truly they represent, in the phrase of Henry James, "a realized ideal" and a study of them should reveal that ideal. From such a study we can only conclude that it is life without effort or responsibility, with every physical need luxuriously gratified. But these hotels nevertheless represent democracy, it may be urged, for the reason that every one may there buy board and lodging and mercenary service if he has the price. The exceeding greatness of that price, however, makes of it a badge of nobility which converts these democratic hostelries into feudal castles, more inaccessible to the Long Denied than as though entered by a drawbridge and surrounded by a moat.

We need not even glance at the churches, for the tides of our spiritual life flow no longer in full volume through their portals; neither may the colleges long detain us, for architecturally considered they give forth a confusion of tongues which has its analogue in the confusion of ideas in the collective academic head.

Is our search for some sign of democracy ended, and is it vain? No, democracy exists in the secret heart of the people, all the people, but it is a thing so new, so strange, so secret and sacred—the ideal of brotherhood—that it is unmanifest yet in time and space. It is a thing born not with the Declaration of Independence, but only yesterday, with the call to a new crusade. The National Army is its cradle, and it is nurtured wherever communities unite to serve the sacred cause. Although menaced by the bloody sword of Imperialism in Europe, it perhaps stands in no less danger from the secret poison of graft and greed and treachery here at home. But it is a spiritual birth, and therefore it cannot perish, but will live to write itself on space in terms of beauty such as the world has never known.

II

DURING THE WAR

The best thing that can be said about our immediate architectural past is that it is past, for it has contributed little of value to an architecture of democracy. During that neo-feudal period the architect prospered, having his place at the baronial table; but now poor Tom's a-cold on a war-swept heath, with food only for reflection. This is but natural; the architect, in so far as he is an artist, is a purveyor of beauty; and the abnormal conditions inevitable to a state of war are devastating to so feminine and tender a thing, even though war be the very soil from which new beauty springs. With Mars in mid-heaven how afflicted is the horoscope of all artists! The skilled hand of the musician is put to coarser uses; the eye that learned its lessons from the sunset must learn the trick of making invisible warships and great guns. Let the architect serve the war-god likewise, in any capacity that offers, confident that this troubling of the waters will bring about a new precipitation; that once the war is over, men will turn from those "old, unhappy, far-off things" to pastures beautiful and new.

In whatever way the war may complicate the architect's personal problem, it should simplify and clarify his attitude toward his art. With no matter what seriousness and sincerity he may have undertaken his personal search for truth and beauty, he will come to question, as never before, both its direction and its results. He is bound to perceive, if he does not perceive already, that the war's arrestment of architecture (in all but its most utilitarian and ephemeral phases) is no great loss to the world for the reason that our architecture was uninspired, unoriginal, done without joy, without reverence, without conviction: a thing which any wind of a new spirit was bound to make appear foolish to a generation with sight rendered clairvoyant through its dedication to great and regenerative ends.

He will come to perceive that between the Civil War and the crusade that is now upon us, we were under the evil spell of materialism. Now materialism is the very negation of democracy, which is a government by the *demos*, or over-soul; it is equally the negation of joy, the negation of reverence, and it is without conviction because it cannot believe even in itself. Reflecting thus, he can scarcely fail to realize that materialism, everywhere entrenched, was entrenched strongest in the camps of the rich—not the idle rich, for materialism is so terrible a taskmaster that it makes its votaries its slaves. These slaves, in turn, made a slave of the artist, a minister to their pride and pretence. His art thus lacked that "sad sincerity" which alone might have saved it in a crisis. When the storm broke militant democracy turned to the engineer, who produced buildings at record speed, by the mile, with only such architectural assistance as could be first and easiest fished up from the dragnet of the draft.

In one direction only does there appear to be open water. Toward the general housing problem the architectural profession has been spurred into activity by reason of the war, and to its credit be it said, it is now thoroughly aroused. The American Institute of Architects sent a commissioner to England to study housing in its latest manifestations, and some of the ablest and most influential members of that organization have placed their services at the disposal of the government. Moreover, there is a manifest disposition, on the part of architects everywhere, to help in this matter all they can. The danger dwells in the possibility that their advice will not be heeded, their services not be fully utilized, but through chicanery, ignorance, or inanition, we will relapse into the tentative, "expensively provisional" methods which have governed the housing of workers hitherto. Even so, architects will doubtless recapture, and more than recapture, their imperiled prestige, but under what changed conditions, and with what an altered attitude toward their art and their craft!

They will find that they must unlearn certain things the schools had taught them: preoccupation with the relative merits of Gothic and Classic—tweedledum and tweedledee. Furthermore, they must learn certain neglected lessons from the engineer, lessons that they will be able immeasurably to better, for although the engineer is a very monster of competence and efficiency within his limits, these are sharply marked, and to any detailed knowledge of that "beautiful necessity" which determines spatial rhythm and counterpoint he is a stranger. The ideal relation between architect and engineer is that of a happily wedded pair—strength married to beauty; in the period just passed or passing they have been as disgruntled divorcés.

The author has in mind one child of such a happy union brought about by the war; the building is the Red Cross Community Club House at Camp Sherman, which, in the pursuit of his destiny, and for the furtherance of his education, he inhabited for two memorable weeks. He learned there more lessons than a few, and encountered more tangled skeins of destiny than he is ever likely to unravel. The matter has so direct a bearing, both on the subject of architecture and of democracy, that it is worth discussing at some length.

This club house stands, surrounded by its tributary dormitories, on a government reservation, immediately adjacent to the camp itself, the whole constituting what is known as the Community Center. By the payment of a dollar any soldier is free to entertain his relatives and friends there, and it is open to all the soldiers at all times. Because the iron discipline of the army is relaxed as soon as the limits of the camp are overpassed, the atmosphere is favourable to social life.

The building occupies its acre of ground invitingly, though exteriorly of no particular distinction. It is the interior that entitles it to consideration as a contribution to an architecture of that new-born democracy of which our army camps have been the cradle. The plan of this interior is cruciform, two hundred feet in each dimension. Built by the Red Cross of the state of Ohio, and dedicated to the larger uses of that organization, the symbolic appropriateness of this particular geometrical figure should not pass unremarked. The cross is divided into side aisles, nave, and crossing, with galleries and mezzanines so arranged as to shorten the arms of the cross in its upper stages, leaving the clear-story surrounding the crossing unimpeded and well defined. The light comes for the most part from high windows, filtering down, in tempered brightness to the floor. The bones of the structure are everywhere in evidence, and an element of its beauty, by reason of the admirably direct and logical arrangement of posts and trusses. The vertical walls are covered with plaster-board of a light buff color, converted into good sized panels by means of wooden strips finished with a thin grey stain. The structural wood work is stained in similar fashion, the iron rods, straps, and bolts being painted black. This color scheme is completed and a little enlivened by red stripes and crosses placed at appropriate intervals in the general design.

The building attained its final synthesis through the collaboration of a Cleveland architect and a National Army captain of engineers. It is so single in its appeal that one does not care to inquire too closely into the part of each in the performance; both are in evidence, for an architect seldom succeeds in being so direct and simple, while an engineer seldom succeeds in being so gracious and altogether suave.

Entirely aside from its æsthetic interest—based as this is on beauty of organism almost alone—the building is notable for the success with which it fulfils and co-ordinates its manifold functions: those of a dormitory, a restaurant, a ballroom, a theatre, and a lounge. The arm of the cross containing the principal entrance accommodates the office, coat room, telephones, news and cigar stand, while leaving the central nave unimpeded, so that from the door one gets the unusual effect of an interior vista two hundred feet long. The restaurant occupies the entire left transept, with a great brick fireplace at the far end. There is another fireplace in the centre of the side of the arm beyond the crossing; that part which would correspond in a cathedral to the choir and apse being given over to the uses of a reading and writing room. The right transept forms a theatre, on occasion, terminating as it does with a stage. The central floor spaces are kept everywhere free except in the restaurant, the sides and angles being filled in with leather-covered sofas, wicker and wooden chairs and tables, arranged in groups favourable to comfort and conversation. Two stairways, at the right and left of the restaurant, give access to the ample balcony and to the bedrooms, which occupy three of the four ends of the arms of the cross at this level.

The appearance and atmosphere of this great interior is inspiring; particularly of an evening, when it is thronged with soldiers, and civilian guests. The strains of music, the hum of many voices, the rhythmic shuffle on the waxed floor of the feet of the dancers—these eminently social sounds mingle and lose themselves in the spaces of the roof, like the voice of many waters. Tobacco smoke ascends like incense, blue above the prevailing green-brown of the crowd, shot here and there with brighter colors from the women's hats and dresses, in the kaleidoscopic shifting of the dance. Long parallel rows of orange lights, grouped low down on the lofty pillars, reflect themselves on the polished floor, and like the patina of time on painted canvas impart to the entire animated picture an incomparable tone. For the lighting, either by accident or by inspiration, is an achievement of the happiest, an example of the friendliness of fate to him who attempts a free solution of his problem. The brackets consist merely of a cruciform arrangement of planed pine boards about each column, with the end grain painted red. On the under side of each arm of the cross is a single electric bulb enclosed within an orange-coloured shade to kill the glare. The light makes the bare wood of the fixture appear incandescent, defining its geometry in rose colour with the most beautiful effect.

The club house is the centre of the social and ceremonial life of the camp, for balls, dinners, receptions, conferences, concerts without number; and it has been the scene of a military wedding—the daughter of a major-general to the grandson of an ex-president. To these events the unassuming, but pervasive beauty of the place lends a dignity new to our social life. In our army camps social life is truly democratic, as any one who has experienced it does not need to be told. Not alone have the conditions of conscription conspired to make it so, but there is a manifest *will-to-democracy*—the growing of a new flower of the spirit, sown in a community of sacrifice, to reach its maturity, perhaps, only in a community of suffering.

The author may seem to have over-praised this Community Club House; with the whole country to draw from for examples it may well appear fatuous to concentrate the reader's attention, for so long, on a building in a remote part of the Middle West: cheap, temporary, and requiring only twenty-one days for its erection. But of the transvaluation of values brought about by the war, this building is an eminent example: it stands in symbolic relation to the times; it represents what may be called the architecture of Service; it is among the first of the new temples of the new democracy, dedicated to the uses of simple, rational social life. Notwithstanding that it fills a felt need, common to every community, there is nothing like it in any of our towns and cities; there are only such poor and partial substitutes as the hotel, the saloon, the dance hall, the lodge room and the club. It is scarcely conceivable that the men and women who have experienced its benefits and its beauty should not demand and have similar buildings in their own home towns.

Beyond the oasis of the Community Club House at Camp Sherman stretch the cantonments—a Euclidian nightmare of bare boards, black roofs and ditches, making grim vistas of straight lines. This is the architecture of Need in contradistinction to the architecture of Greed, symbolized in the shop-window prettiness of those sanitary suburbs of our cities created by the real estate agent and the speculative builder. Neither contain any enduring element of beauty.

But the love of beauty in one form or another exists in every human heart, and if too long or too rigorously denied it finds its own channels of fulfilment. This desire for self-expression through beauty is an important, though little remarked phenomenon of these mid-war times. At the camps it shows itself in the efforts of men of specialized tastes and talents to get together and form dramatic organizations, glee clubs, and orchestras; and more generally by the disposition of the soldiers to sing together at work and play and on the march. The renascence of poetry can be interpreted as a revulsion against the prevailing prosiness; the amateur theatre is equally a protest against the inanity and conventionality of the commercial stage; while the Community Chorus movement is an evidence of a desire to escape a narrow professionalism in music. A similar situation has arisen in the field of domestic architecture, in the form of an unorganized, but wide-spread reaction against the cheap and ugly commercialism which has dominated house construction and decoration of the more unpretentious class. This became articulate a few years ago in the large number of books and magazines devoted to house-planning, construction, decoration, furnishing, and garden-craft. The success which has attended these publications, and their marked influence, give some measure of the magnitude of this revolt.

But now attention must be called to a significant, and somewhat sinister fact. The professional in these various fields of æsthetic endeavour, has shown either indifference or active hostility toward all manner of amateur efforts at self-expression. Free verse aroused the ridicule of the professors of metrics; the Little Theatre movement was solemnly banned by such pundits as Belasco and Mrs. Fiske; the Community Chorus movement has invariably met with opposition and misunderstanding from professional musicians; and with few exceptions the more influential architects have remained aloof from the effort to give skilled architectural assistance to those who cannot afford to pay them ten per cent.

Thus everywhere do we discover a deadening hand laid upon the self-expression of the democratic spirit through beauty. Its enemies are of its own household; those who by nature and training should be its helpers hinder it instead. Why do they do this? Because their fastidious, æsthetic natures are outraged by a crudeness which they themselves could easily refine away if they chose; because also they recoil at a lack of conformity to existing conventions—conventions so hampering to the inner spirit of the Newness, that in order to incarnate at all it must of necessity sweep them aside.

But in every field of æsthetic endeavour appears here and there a man or a woman with unclouded vision, who is able to see in the flounderings of untrained amateurs the stirrings of *demos* from his age-long sleep. These, often forsaking paths more profitable, lend their skilled assistance, not seeking to impose the ancient outworn forms upon the Newness, but by a transfusion of consciousness permitting it to create forms of its own. Such a one, in architecture, Louis Sullivan has proved himself; in music Harry Barnhart, who evokes the very spirit of song from any random crowd. The *demos* found voice first in the poetry of Walt Whitman who has a successor in Vachel Lindsay, the man who walked through Kansas, trading poetry for food and lodging, teaching the farmers' sons and daughters to intone his stirring odes to Pocahontas, General Booth, and Old John Brown. Isadora Duncan, Gordon Craig, Maeterlinck, Scriabine are perhaps too remote from the spirit of democracy, too tinged with old-world æstheticism, to be included in this particular category, but all are image-breakers, liberators, and have played their part in the preparation of the field for an art of democracy.

To the architect falls the task, in the new dispensation, of providing the appropriate material environment for its new life. If he holds the old ideas and cherishes the old convictions current before the war he can do nothing but reproduce their forms and fashions; for architecture, in the last analysis, is only the handwriting of consciousness on space, and materialism has written there already all that it has to tell of its failure to satisfy the mind and heart of man. However beautiful old forms may seem to him they will declare their inadequacy to generations free of that mist of familiarity which now makes life obscure. If, on the other hand, submitting himself to the inspiration of the *demos* he experiences a change of consciousness, he will become truly and newly creative.

His problem, in other words, is not to interpret democracy in terms of existing idioms, be they classic or romantic, but to experience democracy in his heart and let it create and determine its new forms through him. It is not for him to *impose*, it is for him to be *imposed upon*.

"The passive Master lent his hand
   To the vast soul that o'er him planned"

says Emerson in *The Problem*, a poem, which seems particularly addressed to architects, and which every one of them would do well to learn by heart.

If he is at a loss to know where to go and what to do in order to be played upon by these great forces let him direct his attention to the army and the army camps. Here the spirit of democracy is already incarnate. These soldiers, violently shaken free from their environment, stripped of all but the elemental necessities of life; facing a sinister destiny beyond a human-shark-infested ocean, are today the fortunate of earth by reason of their realization of brotherhood, not as a beautiful theory, but as a blessed fact of experience. They will come back with ideas that they cannot utter, with memories that they cannot describe; they will have dreamed dreams and seen visions, and their hearts will stir to potencies for which materialism has not even a name.

The future of the country will be in their young hands. Will they re-create, from its ruins, the faithless and loveless feudalism from which the war set them free? No, they will seek only for self-expression, the expression of that aroused and indwelling spirit which shall create the new, the true democracy. And because it is a spiritual thing it will come clothed in beauty; that is, it will find its supreme expression through the forms of art. The architect who assists in the emprise of weaving this garment will be supremely blessed, but only he who has kept the vigil with prayer and fasting will be supremely qualified.

III

AFTER THE WAR

"When the old world is sterile
 And the ages are effete,
 He will from wrecks and sediment
 The fairer world complete."

The World Soul. Emerson.

He whom the World Soul "forbids to despair" cannot but hope; and he who hopes tries ever to imagine that "fairer world" yearning for birth beyond this interval of blood and tears. Prophecy, to all but the anointed, is dangerous and uncertain, but even so, the author cannot forbear attempting to prevision the architecture likely to arise from the wrecks and sediment left by the war. As a basis for this forecast it is necessary first of all briefly to classify the expression of the building impulse from what may be called the psychological point of view.

Broadly speaking, there are not five orders of architecture—nor fifty—but only two: *Arranged* and *Organic*. These correspond to the two terms of that "inevitable duality" which bisects life. Talent and genius, reason and intuition, bromide and sulphite are some of the names we know them by.

Arranged architecture is reasoned and artificial; produced by talent, governed by taste. Organic architecture, on the other hand, is the product of some obscure inner necessity for self-expression which is sub-conscious. It is as though Nature herself, through some human organ of her activity, had addressed herself to the service of the sons and daughters of men.

Arranged architecture in its finest manifestations is the product of a pride, a knowledge, a competence, a confidence staggering to behold. It seems to say of the works of Nature, "I'll show you a trick worth two of that." For the subtlety of Nature's geometry, and for her infinite variety and unexpectedness, Arranged architecture substitutes a Euclidian system of straight lines and (for the most part) circular curves, assembled and arranged according to a definite logic of its own. It is created but not creative; it is imagined but not imaginative. Organic architecture is both creative and imaginative. It is non-Euclidian in the sense that it is higher-dimensional—that is, it suggests extension in directions and into regions where the spirit finds itself at home, but of which the senses give no report to the brain.

To make the whole thing clearer it may be said that Arranged and Organic architecture bear much the same relation to one another that a piano bears to a violin. A piano is an instrument that does not give forth discords if one follows the rules. A violin requires absolutely an ear—an inner rectitude. It has a way of betraying the man of talent and glorifying the genius, becoming one with his body and his soul.

Of course it stands to reason that there is not always a hard and fast differentiation between these two orders of architecture, but there is one sure way by which each may be recognized and known. If the function appears to have created the form, and if everywhere the form follows the function, changing as that changes, the building is Organic; if on the contrary, "the house confines the spirit," if the building presents not a face but however beautiful a mask, it is an example of Arranged architecture.

The Gothic cathedrals of the "Heart of Europe"—now the place of Armageddon—represent the most perfect and powerful incarnation of the Organic spirit in architecture. After the decadence of mediaeval feudalism—synchronous with that of monasticism—the Arranged architecture of the Renaissance acquired the ascendant; this was coincident with the rise of humanism, when life became increasingly secular. During the post-Renaissance, or scientific period, of which the war probably marks the close, there has been a confusion of tongues; architecture has spoken only alien or dead languages, learned by rote.

But in so far as it is anything at all, æsthetically, our architecture is Arranged, so if only by the operation of the law of opposites, or alternation, we might reasonably expect the next manifestation to be Organic. There are other and better reasons, however, for such expectancy.

Organic architecture is ever a flower of the religious spirit. When the soul draws near to the surface of life, as it did in the two mystic centuries of the Middle Ages, it *organizes* life; and architecture, along, with the other arts becomes truly creative. The informing force comes not so much *from* man as *through* him. After the war that spirit of brotherhood, born in the camps—as Christ was born in a manger—and bred on the battlefields and in the trenches of Europe, is likely to take on all the attributes of a new religion of humanity, prompting men to such heroisms and renunciations, exciting in them such psychic sublimations, as have characterized the great religious renewals of time past.

If this happens it is bound to write itself on space in an architecture beautiful and new; one which "takes its shape and sun-color" not from the niggardly mind, but from the opulent heart. This architecture will of necessity be organic, the product not of self-assertive personalities, but the work of the "Patient Daemon" organizing the nation into a spiritual democracy.

The author is aware that in this point of view there is little of the "scientific spirit"; but science fails to reckon with the soul. Science advances facing backward, so what prevision can it have of a miraculous and divinely inspired future—or for the matter of that, of any future at all? The old methods and categories will no longer answer; the orderly course of evolution has been violently interrupted by the earthquake of the war; igneous action has superseded aqueous action. The casements of the human mind look out no longer upon familiar hills and valleys, but on a stark, strange, devastated landscape, the ploughed land of some future harvest of the years. It is the end of the Age, the *Kali Yuga*—the completion of a major cycle; but all cycles follow the same sequence: after winter, Spring; and after the Iron Age, the Golden.

The specific features of this organic, divinely inspired architecture of the Golden Age cannot of course be discerned by any one, any more than the manner in which the Great Mystery will present itself anew to consciousness. The most imaginative artist can imagine only in terms of the already-existent; he can speak only the language he has learned. If that language has been derived from mediaevalism, he will let his fancy soar after the manner of Henry Kirby, in his *Imaginative Sketches*; if on the contrary he has learned to think in terms of the classic vernacular, Otto Rieth's *Architectur-Skizzen* will suggest the sort of thing that he is likely to produce. Both results will be as remote as possible from future reality, for the reason that they are so near to present reality. And yet some germs of the future must be enfolded even in the present moment. The course of wisdom is to seek them neither in the old romance nor in the new rationalism, but in the subtle and ever-changing spirit of the times.

The most modern note yet sounded in business, in diplomacy, in social life, is expressed by the phrase, "Live openly!" From every quarter, in regard to every manner of human activity, has come the cry, "Let in the light!" By a physical correspondence not the result of coincidence, but of the operation of an occult law, we have, in a very real sense, let in the light. In buildings of the latest type devoted to large uses, there has been a general abandonment of that "cellular system" of many partitions which produced the pepper-box exterior, in favour of great rooms serving diverse functions lit by vast areas of glass. Although an increase of efficiency has dictated and determined these changes, this breaking down of barriers between human beings and their common sharing of the light of day in fuller measure, is a symbol of the growth of brotherhood, and the search, by the soul, for spiritual light.

Now if this fellowship and this quest gain volume and intensity, its physical symbols are bound to multiply and find ever more perfect forms of manifestation. So both as a practical necessity and as a symbol the most pregnant and profound, we are likely to witness in architecture the development of the House of Light, particularly as human ingenuity has made this increasingly practicable.

Glass is a product still undergoing development, as are also those devices of metal for holding it in position and making the joints weather tight. The accident and fire hazard has been largely overcome by protecting the structural parts, by the use of wire glass, and by other ingenious devices. The author has been informed on good authority that shortly before the outbreak of the war a glass had been invented abroad, and made commercially practicable, which shut out the heat rays, but admitted the light. The use of this glass would overcome the last difficulty—the equalization of temperatures—and might easily result in buildings of an entirely novel type, the approach to which is seen in the "pier and grill" style of exterior. This is being adopted not only for commercial buildings, but for others of widely different function, on account of its manifest advantages. Cass Gilbert's admirable studio apartment at 200 West Fifty-Seventh Street, New York, is a building of this type.

In this seeking for sunlight in our cities, we will come to live on the roofs more and more—in summer in the free air, in winter under variformed shelters of glass. This tendency is already manifesting itself in those newest hotels whose roofs are gardens, convertible into skating ponds, with glazed belvideres for eating in all weathers. Nothing but ignorance and inanition stand in the way of utilization of waste roof spaces. People have lived on the roofs in the past, often enough, and will again.

By shouldering ever upward for air and light, we have too often made of the "downtown" districts cliff-bound canyons—"granite deeps opening into granite deeps." This has been the result of no inherent necessity, but of that competitive greed whose nemesis is ever to miss the very thing it seeks. By intelligent co-operation, backed by legislation, the roads and sidewalks might be made to share the sunlight with the roofs.

This could be achieved in two ways: by stepping back the façades in successive stages—giving top lighting, terraces, and wonderful incidental effects of light and shade—or by adjusting the height of the buildings to the width of their interspaces, making rows of tall buildings alternate with rows of low ones, with occasional fully isolated "skyscrapers" giving variety to the sky-line.

These and similar problems of city planning have been worked out theoretically with much minuteness of detail, and are known to every student of the science of cities, but very little of it all has been realized in a practical way—certainly not on this side of the water, where individual rights are held so sacred that a property owner may commit any kind of an architectural nuisance so long as he confines it to his own front yard. The strength of IS, the weakness of *should be*, conflicting interests and legislative cowardice are responsible for the highly irrational manner in which our cities have grown great.

The search for spiritual light in the midst of materialism finds unconscious symbolization in a way other than this seeking for the sun. It is in the amazing development of artificial illumination. From a purely utilitarian standpoint there is almost nothing that cannot now be accomplished with light, short of making the ether itself luminiferous. The æsthetic development of this field, however, can be said to have scarcely begun. The so recent San Francisco Exposition witnessed the first successful effort of any importance to enhance the effect of architecture by artificial illumination, and to use colored light with a view to its purely pictorial value. Though certain buildings have since been illuminated with excellent effect, it remains true that the corset, chewing-gum, beer and automobile sky signs of our Great White Ways indicate the height to which our imagination has risen in utilizing this Promethean gift in any but necessary ways. Interior lighting, except negatively, has not been dealt with from the standpoint of beauty, but of efficiency; the engineer has preempted this field to the exclusion of the artist.

All this is the result of the atrophy of that faculty to worship and wonder which alone induces the mood from which the creation of beauty springs. Light we regard only as a convenience "to see things by" instead of as the power and glory that it inherently is. Its intense and potent vibrations and the rainbow glory of its colour beat at the door of consciousness in vain. When we awaken to these things we shall organize light into a language of spontaneous emotion, just as from sound music was organized.

It is beside the purpose of this essay to attempt to trace the evolution of this new art form, made possible by modern invention, to indicate what phases it is likely to pass through on the way to what perfections, but that it is bound to add a new glory to architecture is sure. This will come about in two ways: directly, by giving color, quality, subtlety to outdoor and indoor lighting, and indirectly by educating the eye to color values, as the ear has been educated by music; thus creating a need for more color everywhere.

As light is the visible symbol of an inner radiance, so is color the sign manual of happiness, of joy. Our cities are so dun and drab in their outward aspects, by reason of the weight of care that burdens us down. We decry the happy irresponsibility of the savage, and the patient contentment of the Oriental with his lot, but both are able to achieve marvels of color in their environment beyond the compass of civilized man. The glory of mediaeval cathedral windows is a still living confutation of the belief that in those far-off times the human heart was sad. Architecture is the index of the inner life of those who produced it, and whenever it is colorful that inner life contains an inner joy.

In the coming Golden Age life will be joyous, and if it is joyous, colour will come into architecture again. Our psychological state even now, alone prevents it, for we are rich in materials and methods to make such polychromy possible. In an article in a recent number of *The Architectural Record*, Mr. Leon V. Solon, writing from an entirely different point of view, divines this tendency, and expresses the opinion that color is again renascent. This tendency is so marked, and this opinion is so shared that we may look with confidence toward a color-evolution in architectural art.

The question of the character of what may be called the ornamental mode of the architecture of the New Age is of all questions the most obscure. Evolution along the lines of the already existent does not help us here, for we are utterly without any ornamental mode from which a new and better might conceivably evolve. Nothing so betrays the spiritual bankruptcy of the end of the Iron Age as this.

The only light on this problem which we shall find, dwells in the realm of metaphysics rather than in the world of material reality. Ornament, more than any other element of architecture, is deeply psychological, it is an externalization of an inner life. This is so true that any time-worn fragment out of the past when art was a language can usually be assigned to its place and its period, so eloquent is it of a particular people and a particular time. Could we therefore detect and understand the obscure movement of consciousness in the modern world, we might gain some clue to the language it would later find.

It is clear that consciousness is moving away from its absorption in materiality because it is losing faith in materialism. Clairvoyance, psychism, the recrudescence of mysticism, of occultism—these signs of the times are straws which show which way the wind now sets, and indicate that the modern mind is beginning to find itself at home in what is called *the fourth dimension*. The phrase is used here in a different sense from that in which the mathematician uses it, but oddly enough four-dimensional geometry provides the symbols by which some of these occult and mystical ideas may be realized by the rational mind. One of the most engaging and inspiring of these ideas is that the personal self is a *projection* on the plane of materiality of a metaphysical self, or soul, to which the personal self is related as is the shadow of an object to the object itself. Now this coincides remarkably with the idea implicit in all higher-space speculation, that the figures of solid geometry are projections on a space of three dimensions, of corresponding four-dimensional forms.

All ornament is in its last analysis geometrical—sometimes directly so, as in the system developed by the Moors. Will the psychology of the new dispensation find expression through some adaptation of four-dimensional geometry? The idea is far from absurd, by reason of the decorative quality inherent in many of the regular hypersolids of four-dimensional space when projected upon solid and plane space.

If this suggestion seems too fanciful, there is still recourse to the law of analogy in finding the thing we seek. Every fresh religious impulse has always developed a symbology through which its truths are expressed and handed down. These symbols, woven into the very texture of the life of the people, are embodied by them in their ornamental mode. The sculpture of a Greek temple is a picture-book of Greek religion; the ornamentation of a Gothic cathedral is a veritable bible of the Christian faith. Almost all of the most beautiful and enduring ornaments have first been sacred symbols; the swastika, the "Eye of Buddha," the "Shield of David," the wheel, the lotus, and the cross.

Now that "twilight of the world" following the war perhaps will witness an *Avatara*—the coming of a World-Teacher who will rebuild on the one broad and ancient foundation that temple of Truth which the folly and ignorance of man is ever tearing down. A material counterpart of that temple will in that case afterward arise. Thus will be born the architecture of the future; and the ornament of that architecture will tell, in a new set of symbols, the story of the rejuvenation of the world.

In this previsioning of architecture after the war, the author must not be understood to mean that these things will be realized *directly* after. Architecture, from its very nature, is the most sluggish of all the arts to respond to the natural magic of the quick-moving mind—it is Caliban, not Ariel. Following the war the nation will be for a time depleted of man-power, burdened with debt, prostrate, exhausted. But in that time of reckoning will come reflection, penitence.

"And I'll be wise hereafter,
  And seek for grace. What a thrice-double ass
  Was I, to take this drunkard for a god,
  And worship this dull fool."

With some such epilogue the curtain will descend on the great drama now approaching a close. It will be for the younger generations, the reincarnate souls of those who fell in battle, to inaugurate the work of giving expression, in deathless forms of art, to the vision of that "fairer world" glimpsed now only as by lightning, in a dream.

ESSAYS

ORNAMENT FROM MATHEMATICS

I

THE WORLD ORDER

No fact is better established than that we live in an *orderly* universe. The truth of this the world-war may for the moment, and to the near and narrow view appear to contradict, but the sweep of human history, and the stars in their courses, show an orderliness which cannot be gainsaid.

Now of that order, *number*—that is, mathematics—is the more than symbol, it is the very thing itself. Whence this weltering tide of life arose, and whither it flows, we know not; but that it is governed by mathematical law all of our knowledge in every field confirms. Were it not so, knowledge itself would be impossible. It is because man is a counting animal that he is master over all the beasts of the earth.

Number is the tune to which all things move, and as it were make music; it is in the pulses of the blood no less than in the starred curtain of the sky. It is a necessary concomitant alike of the sharp bargain, the chemical experiment, and the fine frenzy of the poet. Music is number made audible; architecture is number made visible; nature geometrizes not alone in her crystals, but in her most intricate arabesques.

If number be indeed the universal solvent of all forms, sounds, motions, may we not make of it the basis of a new æsthetic—a loom on which to weave patterns the like of which the world has never seen? To attempt such a thing—to base art on mathematics—argues (some one is sure to say) an entire misconception of the nature and function of art. "Art is a fountain of spontaneous emotion"—what, therefore, can it have in common with the proverbially driest, least spontaneous preoccupation of the human mind? But the above definition concludes with the assertion that this emotion reaches the soul "through various channels." The transit can be effected only through some sensuous element, some language (in the largest sense), and into this the element of number and form must inevitably enter—mathematics is "there" and cannot be thought or argued away.

But to make mathematics, and not the emotion which it expresses, the important thing, is not this to fall into the time-worn heresy of art for art's sake, that is, art for form's sake—art for the sake of mathematics? To this objection there is an answer, and as this answer contains the crux of the whole matter, embraces the proposition by which this thesis must stand or fall, it must be full and clear.

What is it, in the last analysis, that all art which is not purely personal and episodical strives to express? Is it not the *world-order*?—the very thing that religion, philosophy, science, strive according to their different natures and methods to express? The perception of the world-order by the artist arouses an emotion to which he can give vent only in terms of number; but number is itself the most abstract expression of the world order. The form and content of art are therefore not different, but the same. A deep sense of this probably inspired Pater's famous saying that all art aspires toward the condition of music; for music, from its very nature, is the world-order uttered in terms of number, in a sense and to a degree not attained by any other art.

This is not mere verbal juggling. We have suffered so long from an art-phase which exalts the personal, as opposed to the cosmic, that we have lost sight of the fact that the great arts of antiquity, preceding the Renaissance, insisted on the cosmic, or impersonal aspect, and on this alone, just as does Oriental art, even today. The secret essence, the archetypal idea of the subject is the preoccupation of the Oriental artist, as it was of the Egyptian, and of the Greek. We of the West today seek as eagerly to fix the accidental and ephemeral aspect—the shadow of a particular cloud upon a particular landscape; the smile on the face of a specific person, in a recognizable room, at a particular moment of time. Of symbolic art, of universal emotion expressing itself in terms which are universal, we have very little to show.

The reason for this is first, our love for, and understanding of, the concrete and personal: it is the *world-aspect* and not the *world-order* which interests us; and second, the inadequacies of current forms of art expression to render our sense of the eternal secret heart of things as it presents itself to our young eyes. Confronted with this difficulty, we have shirked it, and our ambition has shrunk to the portrayal of those aspects which shuffle our poverty out of sight. It is not a poverty of technique—we are dexterous enough; nor is it a poverty of invention—we are clever enough; it is the poverty of the spiritual bankrupt trying to divert attention by a prodigal display of the smallest of small change.

Reference is made here only to the arts of space; the arts of time—music, poetry, and the (written) drama—employing vehicles more flexible, have been more fortunate, though they too suffer in some degree from worshipping, instead of the god of order, the god of chance.

The corrective of this is a return to first principles: principles so fundamental that they suffer no change, however new and various their illustrations. These principles are embodied in number, and one might almost say nowhere else in such perfection. Mathematics is not the dry and deadly thing that our teaching of it and the uses we put it to have made it seem. Mathematics is the handwriting on the human consciousness of the very Spirit of Life itself. Others before Pythagoras discovered this, and it is the discovery which awaits us too.

To indicate the way in which mathematics might be made to yield the elements of a new æsthetic is beyond the province of this essay, being beyond the compass of its author, but he makes bold to take a single phase: ornament, and to deal with it from this point of view.

The ornament now in common use has been gathered from the dust-bin of the ages. What ornamental *motif* of any universality, worth, or importance is less than a hundred years old? We continue to use the honeysuckle, the acanthus, the fret, the egg and dart, not because they are appropriate to any use we put them to, but because they are beautiful *per se*. Why are they beautiful? It is not because they are highly conventionalized representations of natural forms which are themselves beautiful, but because they express cosmic truths. The honeysuckle and the acanthus leaf, for example, express the idea of successive impulses, mounting, attaining a maximum, and descending—expanding from some focus of force in the manner universal throughout nature. Science recognizes in the spiral an archetypal form, whether found in a whirlpool or in a nebula. A fret is a series of highly conventionalized spirals: translate it from angular to curved and we have the wave-band; isolate it and we have the volute. Egg and dart are phallic emblems, female and male; or, if you prefer, as ellipse and straight line, they are symbols of finite existence contrasted with infinity. [Figure 1.]

Suppose that we determine to divest ourselves of these and other precious inheritances, not because they have lost their beauty and meaning, but rather on account of their manifold associations with a past which the war makes suddenly more remote than slow centuries have done; suppose that we determine to supplant these symbols with others no less charged with beauty and meaning, but more directly drawn from the inexhaustible well of mathematical truth—how shall we set to work?

We need not *set* to work, because we have done that already, we are always doing it, unknowingly, and without knowing the reason why. All ornamentalists are subjective mathematicians—an amazing statement, perhaps, but one susceptible of confirmation in countless amusing ways, of which two will be shown.

Consider first your calendar—your calendar whose commonplace face, having yielded you information as to pay day, due day, and holiday, you obliterate at the end of each month without a qualm, oblivious to the fact that were your interests less sordid and personal it would speak to you of that order which pervades the universe; would make you realize something of the music of the spheres. For on that familiar checkerboard of the days are numerical arrangements which are mysterious, "magical"; each separate number is as a spider at the center of an amazing mathematical web. That is to say, every number is discovered to be half of the sum of the pairs of numbers which surround it, vertically, horizontally, and diagonally: all of the pairs add to the same sum, and the central number divides this sum by two. A graphic indication of this fact on the calendar face by means of a system of intersecting lines yields that form of classic grille dear to the heart of every tyro draughtsman. [Figure 2.] Here is an evident relation between mathematical fact and ornamental mode, whether the result of accident, or by reason of some subconscious connection between the creative and the reasoning part of the mind.

To show, by means of an example other than this acrostic of the days, how the pattern-making instinct follows unconsciously in the groove traced out for it by mathematics, the attention of the reader is directed to the design of the old Colonial bed-spread shown in Figure 3. Adjacent to this, in the upper right hand corner, is a magic square of four. That is, all of the columns of figures of which it is composed: vertical, horizontal and diagonal add to the same sum: 34. An analysis of this square reveals the fact that it is made up of the figures of two different orders of counting: the ordinary order, beginning at the left hand upper corner and reading across and down in the usual way, and the reverse-ordinary, beginning at the lower right hand corner and reading across and up. The figures in the four central cells and in the four outside corner cells are discovered to belong in the first category, and the remaining figures in the second. Now if the ordinary order cells be represented by white, and the reverse ordinary by black, just such a pattern has been created as forms the decorative motif of the quilt.

It may be claimed that these two examples of a relation between ornament and mathematics are accidental and therefore prove nothing, but they at least furnish a clue which the artist would be foolish not to follow up. Let him attack his problem this time directly, and see if number may not be made to yield the thing he seeks: namely, space-rhythms which are beautiful and new.

We know that there is a beauty inherent in *order*, that necessity of one sort or another is the parent of beauty. Beauty in architecture is largely the result of structural necessity; beauty in ornament may spring from a necessity which is numerical. It is clear that the arrangement of numbers in a magic square is necessitous—they must be placed in a certain way in order that the summation of every column shall be the same. The problem then becomes to make that necessity reveal itself to the eye. Now most magic squares contain a *magic path*, discovered by following the numbers from cell to cell in their natural order. Because this is a necessitous line it should not surprise us that it is frequently beautiful as well.

The left hand drawing in Figure 4 represents the smallest aggregation of numbers that is capable of magic square arrangement. Each vertical, horizontal, and corner diagonal column adds up to 15, and the sum of any two opposite numbers is 10, which is twice the center number. The magic path is the endless line developed by following, free hand, the numbers in their natural order, from 1 to 9 and back to 1 again. The drawing at the right of Figure 4 is this same line translated into ornament by making an interlace of it, and filling in the larger interstices with simple floral forms. This has been executed in white plaster and made to perform the function of a ventilating grille.

Now the number of magic squares is practically limitless, and while all of them do not yield magic lines of the beauty of this one, some contain even richer decorative possibilities. But there are also other ways of deriving ornament from magic squares, already hinted at in the discussion of the Colonial quilt.

Magic squares of an even number of cells are found sometimes to consist of numbers arranged not only in combinations of the ordinary and the reverse ordinary orders of counting, but involving two others as well: the reverse of the ordinary (beginning at the upper right hand, across, and down) and the reversed inverse, (beginning at the lower left hand, across, and up). If, in such a magic square, a simple graphic symbol be substituted for the numbers belonging to each order, pattern spontaneously springs to life. Figures 5 and 6 exemplify the method, and Figures 7 and 8 the translation of some of these squares into richer patterns by elaborating the symbols while respecting their arrangement. By only a slight stretch of the imagination the beautiful pierced stone screen from Ravenna shown in Figure 9 might be conceived of as having been developed according to this method, although of course it was not so in fact. Some of the arrangements shown in Figure 6 are closely paralleled in the acoustic figures made by means of musical tones with sand, on a sheet of metal or glass.

The celebrated Franklin square of 16 cells can be made to yield a beautiful pattern by designating some of the lines which give the summation of 2056 by different symbols, as shown in Figure 10. A free translation of this design into pattern brickwork is indicated in Figure 11.

If these processes seem unduly involved and elaborate for the achievement of a simple result—like burning the house down in order to get roast pig—there are other more simple ways of deriving ornament from mathematics, for the truths of number find direct and perfect expression in the figures of geometry. The squaring of a number—the raising of it to its second power—finds graphic expression in the plane figure of the square; and the cubing of a number—the raising of it to its third power—in the solid figure of the cube. Now squares and cubes have been recognized from time immemorial as useful ornamental motifs. Other elementary geometrical figures, making concrete to the eye the truths of abstract number, may be dealt with by the designer in such a manner as to produce ornament the most varied and profuse. Moorish ceilings, Gothic window tracery, Grolier bindings, all indicate the richness of the field.

Suppose, for example, that we attempt to deal decoratively which such simple figures as the three lowest Platonic solids—the tetrahedron, the hexahedron, and the octahedron. [Figure 12.] Their projection on a plane yields a rhythmical division of space, because of their inherent symmetry. These projections would correspond to the network of lines seen in looking through a glass paperweight of the given shape, the lines being formed by the joining of the several faces. Figure 13 represents ornamental bands developed in this manner. The dodecahedron and icosahedron, having more faces, yield more intricate patterns, and there is no limit to the variety of interesting designs obtainable by these direct and simple means.

If the author has been successful thus far in his exposition, it should be sufficiently plain that from the inexhaustible well of mathematics fresh beauty may be drawn. But what of its significance? Ornament must *mean something*; it must have some relation to the dominant ideation of the day; it must express the psychological mood.

What is the psychological mood? Ours is an age of transition; we live in a changing world. On the one hand we witness the breaking up of many an old thought crystal, on the other we feel the pressure of those forces which shall create the new. What is nature's first visible creative act? The formation of a geometrical crystal. The artist should take this hint, and organize geometry into a new ornamental mode; by so doing he will prove himself to be in relation to the *anima mundi*. It is only by the establishment of such a relation that new beauty comes to birth in the world.

Ornament in its primitive manifestations is geometrical rather than naturalistic. This is in a manner strange, that the abstract and metaphysical thing should precede the concrete and sensuous. It would be natural to suppose that man would first imitate the things which surround him, but the most cursory acquaintance with primitive art shows that he is much more apt to crudely geometrize. Now it is not necessary to assume that we are to revert to the conditions of savagery in order to believe that in this matter of a sound æsthetic we must begin where art has always begun—with number and geometry. Nevertheless there is a subtly ironic view which one is justified in holding in regard to quite obvious aspects of American life, in the light of which that life appears to have rather more in common with savagery than with culture.

The submersion of scholarship by athletics in our colleges is a case in point, the contest of muscles exciting much more interest and enthusiasm than any contest of wits. We persist in the savage habit of devouring the corpses of slain animals long after the necessity for it is past, and some even murder innocent wild creatures, giving to their ferocity the name of sport. Our women bedeck themselves with furs and feathers, the fruit of mercenary and systematic slaughter; we perform orgiastic dances to the music of horns and drums and cymbals—in short, we have the savage psychology without its vital religious instinct and its sure decorative sense for color and form.

But this is of course true only of the surface and sunlit shadows of the great democratic tide. Its depths conceal every kind of subtlety and sophistication, high endeavour, and a response to beauty and wisdom of a sort far removed from the amoeba stage of development above sketched. Of this latter stage the simple figures of Euclidian plane and solid geometry—figures which any child can understand—are the appropriate symbols, but for that other more developed state of consciousness—less apparent but more important—these will not do. Something more sophisticated and recondite must be sought for if we are to have an ornamental mode capable of expressing not only the simplicity but the complexity of present-day psychology. This need not be sought for outside the field of geometry, but within it, and by an extension of the methods already described. There is an altogether modern development of the science of mathematics: the geometry of four dimensions. This represents the emancipation of the mind from the tyranny of mere appearances; the turning of consciousness in a new direction. It has therefore a high symbolical significance as typifying that movement away from materialism which is so marked a phenomenon of the times.

Of course to those whose notion of the fourth dimension is akin to that of a friend of the author who described it as "a wagon-load of bung-holes," the idea of getting from it any practical advantage cannot seem anything but absurd. There is something about this form of words "the fourth dimension" which seems to produce a sort of mental-phobia in certain minds, rendering them incapable of perception or reason. Such people, because they cannot stick their cane into it contend that the fourth dimension has no mathematical or philosophical validity. As ignorance on this subject is very general, the following essay will be devoted to a consideration of the fourth dimension and its relation to a new ornamental mode.

II

THE FOURTH DIMENSION

The subject of the fourth dimension is not an easy one to understand. Fortunately the artist in design does not need to penetrate far into these fascinating halls of thought in order to reap the advantage which he seeks. Nevertheless an intention of mind upon this "fairy-tale of mathematics" cannot fail to enlarge his intellectual and spiritual horizons, and develop his imagination—that finest instrument in all his chest of tools.

By way of introduction to the subject Prof. James Byrnie Shaw, in an article in the *Scientific Monthly*, has this to say:

> Up to the period of the Reformation algebraic equations of more than the third degree were frowned upon as having no real meaning, since there is no fourth power or dimension. But about one hundred years ago this chimera became an actual existence, and today it is furnishing a new world to physics, in which mechanics may become geometry, time be co-ordinated with space, and every geometric theorem in the world is a physical theorem in the experimental world in study in the laboratory. Startling indeed it is to the scientist to be told that an artificial dream-world of the mathematician is more real than that he sees with his galvanometers, ultra-microscopes, and spectroscopes. It matters little that he replies, "Your four-dimensional world is only an analytic explanation of my phenomena," for the fact remains a fact, that in the mathematician's four-dimensional space there is a space not derived in any sense of the term as a residue of experience, however powerful a distillation of sensations or perceptions be resorted to, for it is not contained at all in the fluid that experience furnishes. It is a product of the creative power of the mathematical mind, and its objects are real in exactly the same way that the cube, the square, the circle, the sphere or the straight line. We are enabled to see with the penetrating vision of the mathematical insight that no less real and no more real are these fantastic forms of the world of relativity than those supposed to be uncreatable or indestructible in the play of the forces of nature.

These "fantastic forms" alone need concern the artist. If by some potent magic he can precipitate them into the world of sensuous images so that they make music to the eye, he need not even enter into the question of their reality, but in order to achieve this transmutation he should know something, at least, of the strange laws of their being, should lend ear to a fairy-tale in which each theorem is a paradox, and each paradox a mathematical fact.

He must conceive of a space of four mutually independent directions; a space, that is, having a direction at right angles to every direction that we know. We cannot point to this, we cannot picture it, but we can reason about it with a precision that is all but absolute. In such a space it would of course be possible to establish four axial lines, all intersecting at a point, and all mutually at right angles with one another. Every hyper-solid of four-dimensional space has these four axes.

The regular hyper-solids (analogous to the Platonic solids of three-dimensional space) are the "fantastic forms" which will prove useful to the artist. He should learn to lure them forth along them axis lines. That is, let him build up his figures, space by space, developing them from lower spaces to higher. But since he cannot enter the fourth dimension, and build them there, nor even the third—if he confines himself to a sheet of paper—he must seek out some form of *representation* of the higher in the lower. This is a process with which he is already acquainted, for he employs it every time he makes a perspective drawing, which is the representation of a solid on a plane. All that is required is an extension of the method: a hyper-solid can be represented in a figure of three dimensions, and this in turn can be projected on a plane. The achieved result will constitute a perspective of a perspective—the representation of a representation.

This may sound obscure to the uninitiated, and it is true that the plane projection of some of the regular hyper-solids are staggeringly intricate affairs, but the author is so sure that this matter lies so well within the compass of the average non-mathematical mind that he is willing to put his confidence to a practical test.

It is proposed to develop a representation of the tesseract or hyper-cube on the paper of this page, that is, on a space of two dimensions. Let us start as far back as we can: with a point. This point, a, [Figure 14] is conceived to move in a direction w, developing the line a b. This line next moves in a direction at right angles to w, namely, x, a distance equal to its length, forming the square a b c d. Now for the square to develop into a cube by a movement into the third dimension it would have to move in a direction at right angles to both w and x, that is, out of the plane of the paper—away from it altogether, either up or down. This is not possible, of course, but the third direction can be *represented* on the plane of the paper.

Let us represent it as diagonally downward toward the right, namely, y. In the y direction, then, and at a distance equal to the length of one of the sides of the square, another square is drawn, a'b'c'd', representing the original square at the end of its movement into the third dimension; and because in that movement the bounding points of the square have traced out lines (edges), it is necessary to connect the corresponding corners of the two squares by means of lines. This completes the figure and achieves the representation of a cube on a plane by a perfectly simple and familiar process. Its six faces are easily identified by the eye, though only two of them appear as squares owing to the exigencies of representation.

Now for a leap into the abyss, which won't be so terrifying, since it involves no change of method. The cube must move into the fourth dimension, developing there a hyper-cube. This is impossible, for the reason the cube would have to move out of our space altogether—three-dimensional space will not contain a hyper-cube. But neither is the cube itself contained within the plane of the paper; it is only there *represented*. The y direction had to be imagined and then arbitrarily established; we can arbitrarily establish the fourth direction in the same way. As this is at right angles to y, its indication may be diagonally downward and to the left—the direction z. As y is known to be at right angles both to w and to x, z is at right angles to all three, and we have thus established the four mutually perpendicular axes necessary to complete the figure.

The cube must now move in the z direction (the fourth dimension) a distance equal to the length of one of its sides. Just as we did previously in the case of the square, we draw the cube in its new position (ABB'D'C'C) and also as before we connect each apex of the first cube with the corresponding apex of the other, because each of these points generates a line (an edge), each line a plane, and each plane a solid. This is the tesseract or hyper-cube in plane projection. It has the 16 points, 32 lines, and 8 cubes known to compose the figure. These cubes occur in pairs, and may be readily identified.[1]

The tesseract as portrayed in A, Figure 14, is shown according to the conventions of oblique, or two-point perspective; it can equally be represented in a manner correspondent to parallel perspective. The parallel perspective of a cube appears as a square inside another square, with lines connecting the four vertices of the one with those of the other. The third dimension (the one beyond the plane of the paper) is here conceived of as being not beyond the boundaries of the first square, but *within* them. We may with equal propriety conceive of the fourth dimension as a "beyond which is within." In that case we would have a rendering of the tesseract as shown in B, Figure 14: a cube within a cube, the space between the two being occupied by six truncated pyramids, each representing a cube. The large outside cube represents the original generating cube at the beginning of its motion into the fourth dimension, and the small inside cube represents it at the end of that motion.

These two projections of the tesseract upon plane space are not the only ones possible, but they are typical. Some idea of the variety of aspects may be gained by imagining how a nest of inter-related cubes (made of wire, so as to interpenetrate), combined into a single symmetrical figure of three-dimensional space, would appear from several different directions. Each view would yield new space-subdivisions, and all would be rhythmical—susceptible, therefore, of translation into ornament. C and D represent such translations of A and B.

In order to fix these unfamiliar ideas more firmly in the reader's mind, let him submit himself to one more exercise of the creative imagination, and construct, by a slightly different method, a representation of a hexadecahedroid, or 16-hedroid, on a plane. This regular solid of four-dimensional space consists of sixteen cells, each a regular tetrahedron, thirty-two triangular faces, twenty-four edges and eight vertices. It is the correlative of the octahedron of three-dimensional space.

First it is necessary to establish our four axes, all mutually at right angles. If we draw three lines intersecting at a point, subtending angles of 60 degrees each, it is not difficult to conceive of these lines as being at right angles with one another in three-dimensional space. The fourth axis we will assume to pass vertically through the point of intersection of the three lines, so that we see it only in cross-section, that is, as a point. It is important to remember that all of the angles made by the four axes are right angles—a thing possible only in a space of four dimensions. Because the 16-hedroid is a symmetrical hyper-solid all of its eight apexes will be equidistant from the centre of a containing hyper-sphere, whose "surface" these will intersect at symmetrically disposed points. These apexes are established in our representation by describing a circle—the plane projection of the hyper-sphere—about the central point of intersection of the axes. (Figure 15, left.) Where each of these intersects the circle an apex of the 16-hedroid will be established. From each apex it is now necessary to draw straight lines to every other, each line representing one edge of the sixteen tetrahedral cells. But because the two ends of the fourth axis are directly opposite one another, and opposite the point of sight, all of these lines fail to appear in the left hand diagram. It therefore becomes necessary to *tilt* the figure slightly, bringing into view the fourth axis, much foreshortened, and with it, all of the lines which make up the figure. The result is that projection of the 16-hedroid shown at the right of Figure 15.[2] Here is no fortuitous arrangement of lines and areas, but the "shadow" cast by an archetypal, figure of higher space upon the plane of our materiality. It is a wonder, a mystery, staggering to the imagination, contradictory to experience, but as well entitled to a place at the high court of reason as are any of the more familiar figures with which geometry deals. Translated into ornament it produces such an all-over pattern as is shown in Figure 16 and the design which adorns the curtains at right and left of pl. XIII. There are also other interesting projections of the 16-hedroid which need not be gone into here.

For if the author has been successful in his exposition up to this point, it should be sufficiently plain that the geometry of four-dimensions is capable of yielding fresh and interesting ornamental motifs. In carrying his demonstration farther, and in multiplying illustrations, he would only be going over ground already covered in his book *Projective Ornament* and in his second Scammon lecture.

Of course this elaborate mechanism for producing quite obvious and even ordinary decorative motifs may appear to some readers like Goldberg's nightmare mechanics, wherein the most absurd and intricate devices are made to accomplish the most simple ends. The author is undisturbed by such criticisms. If the designs dealt with in this chapter are "obvious and even ordinary" they are so for the reason that they were chosen less with an eye to their interest and beauty than as lending themselves to development and demonstration by an orderly process which should not put too great a tax upon the patience and intelligence of the reader. Four-dimensional geometry yields numberless other patterns whose beauty and interest could not possibly be impeached—patterns beyond the compass of the cleverest designer unacquainted with projective geometry.

The great need of the ornamentalist is this or some other solid foundation. Lacking it, he has been forced to build either on the shifting sands of his own fancy, or on the wrecks and sediment of the past. Geometry provides this sure foundation. We may have to work hard and dig deep, but the results will be worth the effort, for only on such a foundation can arise a temple which is beautiful and strong.

In confirmation of his general contention that the basis of all effective decoration is geometry and number, the author, in closing, desires to direct the reader's attention to Figure 17 a slightly modified rendering of the famous zodiacal ceiling of the Temple of Denderah, in Egypt. A sun and its corona have been substituted for the zodiacal signs and symbols which fill the centre of the original, for except to an Egyptologist these are meaningless. In all essentials the drawing faithfully follows the original—was traced, indeed, from a measured drawing.

Here is one of the most magnificent decorative schemes in the whole world, arranged with a feeling for balance and rhythm exceeding the power of the modern artist, and executed with a mastery beyond the compass of a modern craftsman. The fact that first forces itself upon the beholder is that the thing is so obviously mathematical in its rhythms, that to reduce it to terms of geometry and number is a matter of small difficulty. Compare the frozen music of these rhymed and linked figures with the herded, confused, and cluttered compositions of even our best decorative artists, and argument becomes unnecessary—the fact stands forth that we have lost something precious and vital out of art of which the ancients possessed the secret.

It is for the restoration of these ancient verities and the discovery of new spatial rhythms—made possible by the advance of mathematical science—that the author pleads. Artists, architects, designers, instead of chewing the cud of current fashion, come into these pastures new!

[Footnote 1: The eight cubes in A, Figure 14, are as follows: abb'd'c'c; ABB'D'C'C; abdDCA; a'b'd'D'C'A'; abb'B'A'A; cdd'D'C'C; bb'd'D'DB; aa'c'C'CA.]

[Footnote 2: The sixteen cells of the hexadehahedroid are as follows: ABCD: A'B'C'D': AB'C'D': A'BCD: AB'CD: A'BC'D: ABC'D: A'B'CD': ABCD': A'B'C'D: ABC'D': A'B'CD: A'BC'D: AB'CD': A'BCD': AB'C'D.]

HARNESSING THE RAINBOW

Reference was made in an antecedent essay to an art of light—of mobile color—an abstract language of thought and emotion which should speak to consciousness through the eye, as music speaks through the ear. This is an art unborn, though quickening in the womb of the future. The things that reflect light have been organized æsthetically into the arts of architecture, painting, and sculpture, but light itself has never been thus organized.

And yet the scientific development and control of light has reached a stage which makes this new art possible. It awaits only the advent of the creative artist. The manipulation of light is now in the hands of the illuminating engineers and its exploitation (in other than necessary ways) in the hands of the advertisers.

Some results of their collaboration are seen in the sky signs of upper Broadway, in New York, and of the lake front, in Chicago. A carnival of contending vulgarities, showing no artistry other than the most puerile, these displays nevertheless yield an effect of amazing beauty. This is on account of an occult property inherent in the nature of light—*it cannot be vulgarized*. If the manipulation of light were delivered into the hands of the artist, and dedicated to noble ends, it is impossible to overestimate the augmentation of beauty that would ensue.

For light is a far more potent medium than sound. The sphere of sound is the earth-sphere; the little limits of our atmosphere mark the uttermost boundaries to which sound, even the most strident can possibly prevail. But the medium of light is the ether, which links us with the most distant stars. May not this serve as a symbol of the potency of light to usher the human spirit into realms of being at the doors of which music itself shall beat in vain? Or if we compare the universe accessible to sight with that accessible to sound—the plight of the blind in contrast to that of the deaf—there is the same discrepancy; the field of the eye is immensely richer, more various and more interesting than that of the ear.

The difficulty appears to consist in the inferior impressionability of the eye to its particular order of beauty. To the average man color—as color—has nothing significant to say: to him grass is green, snow is white, the sky blue; and to have his attention drawn to the fact that sometimes grass is yellow, snow blue, and the sky green, is disconcerting rather than illuminating. It is only when his retina is assaulted by some splendid sunset or sky-encircling rainbow that he is able to disassociate the idea of color from that of form and substance. Even the artist is at a disadvantage in this respect, when compared with the musician. Nothing in color knowledge and analysis analogous to the established laws of musical harmony is part of the equipment of the average artist; he plays, as it were, by ear. The scientist, on the other hand, though he may know the spectrum from end to end, and its innumerable modifications, values this "rainbow promise of the Lord" not for its own beautiful sake but as a means to other ends than those of beauty. But just as the art of music has developed the ear into a fine and sensitive instrument of appreciation, so an analogous art of light would educate the eye to nuances of color to which it is now blind.

It is interesting to speculate as to the particular form in which this new art will manifest itself. The question is perhaps already answered in the "color organ," the earliest of which was Bambridge Bishop's, exhibited at the old Barnum's Museum—before the days of electric light—and the latest A.W. Rimington's. Both of these instruments were built upon a supposed correspondence between a given scale of colors, and the musical chromatic scale;

they were played from a musical score upon an organ keyboard. This is sufficiently easy and sufficiently obvious, and has been done, with varying success in one way or another, time and again, but its very ease and obviousness should give us pause.

It may well be questioned whether any arbitrary and literal translation, even though practicable, of a highly complex, intensely mobile art, unfolding in time, as does music, into a correspondent light and color expression, is the best approach to a new art of mobile color. There is a deep and abiding conviction, justified by the history of æsthetics, that each art-form must progress from its own beginnings and unfold in its own unique and characteristic way. Correspondences between the arts—such a correspondence, for example, as inspired the famous saying that architecture is frozen music—reveal themselves usually only after the sister arts have attained an independent maturity. They owe their origin to that underlying unity upon which our various modes of sensuous perception act as a refracting medium, and must therefore be taken for granted. Each art, like each individual, is unique and singular; in this singularity dwells its most thrilling appeal. We are likely to miss light's crowning glory, and the rainbow's most moving message to the soul if we preoccupy ourselves too exclusively with the identities existing between music and color; it is rather their points of difference which should first be dwelt upon.

Let us accordingly consider the characteristic differences between the two sense-categories to which sound and light—music and color—respectively belong. This resolves itself into a comparison between time and space. The characteristic thing about time is succession—hence the very idea of music, which is in time, involves perpetual change. The characteristic of space, on the other hand, is simultaneousness—in space alone perpetual immobility would reign. That is why architecture, which is pre-eminently the art of space, is of all the arts the most static. Light and color are essentially of space, and therefore an art of mobile colour should never lack a certain serenity and repose. A "tune" played on a color organ is only distressing. If there is a workable correspondence between the musical art and an art of mobile color, it will be found in the domain of harmony which involves the idea of simultaneity, rather than in melody, which is pure succession. This fundamental difference between time and space cannot be over-emphasized. A musical note prolonged, becomes at last scarcely tolerable; while a beautiful color, like the blue of the sky, we can enjoy all day and every day. The changing hues of a sunset, are *andante* if referred to a musical standard, but to the eye they are *allegretto*—we would have them pass less swiftly than they do. The winking, chasing, changing lights of illuminated sky-signs are only annoying, and for the same reason. The eye longs for repose in some serene radiance or stately sequence, while the ear delights in contrast and continual change. It may be that as the eye becomes more educated it will demand more movement and complexity, but a certain stillness and serenity are of the very nature of light, as movement and passion are of the very nature of sound. Music is a seeking—"love in search of a word"; light is a finding—a "divine covenant."

With attention still focussed on the differences rather than the similarities between the musical art and a new art of mobile color, we come next to the consideration of the matter of form. Now form is essentially of space: we speak about the "form" of a musical composition, but it is in a more or less figurative and metaphysical sense, not as a thing concrete and palpable, like the forms of space. It would be foolish to forego the advantage of linking up form with colour, as there is opportunity to do. Here is another golden ball to juggle with, one which no art purely in time affords. Of course it is known that musical sounds weave invisible patterns in the air, and to render these patterns perceptible to the eye may be one of the more remote and recondite achievements of our uncreated art. Meantime, though we have the whole treasury of natural forms to draw from, of these we can only properly employ such as are *abstract*. The reason for this is clear to any one who conceives of an art of mobile color, not as a moving picture show—a thing of quick-passing concrete images, to shock, to startle, or to charm—but as a rich and various language in which light, proverbially the symbol of the spirit, is made to speak, through the senses, some healing message to the soul. For such a consummation, "devoutly to be wished," natural forms—forms abounding in every kind of association with that world of materiality from which we would escape—are out of place; recourse must be had rather to abstract forms, that is, geometrical figures. And because the more remote these are from the things of sense, from knowledge and experience, the projected figures of four-dimensional geometry would lend themselves to these uses with an especial grace. Color without form is as a soul without a body; yet the body of light must be without any taint of materiality. Four-dimensional forms are as immaterial as anything that could be imagined and they could be made to serve the useful purpose of separating colors one from another, as lead lines do in old cathedral windows, than which nothing more beautiful has ever been devised.

Coming now to the consideration, not of differences, but similarities, it is clear that a correspondence can be established between the colors of the spectrum and the notes of a musical scale. That is, the spectrum, considered as the analogue of a musical octave can be subdivided into twelve colors which may be representative of the musical chromatic scale of twelve semi-tones: the very word, *chromatic*, being suggestive of such a correspondence between sound and light. The red end of the spectrum would naturally relate to the low notes of the musical scale, and the violet end to the high, by reason of the relative rapidity of vibration in each case; for the octave of a musical note sets the air vibrating twice as rapidly as does the note itself, and roughly speaking, the same is true of the end colors of the spectrum with relation to the ether.

But assuming that a color scale can be established which would yield a color correlative to any musical note or chord, there still remains the matter of *values* to be dealt with. In the musical scale there is a practical equality of values: one note is as potent as another. In a color scale, on the other hand, each note (taken at its greatest intensity) has a positive value of its own, and they are all different. These values have no musical correlatives, they belong to color *per se*. Every colorist knows that the whole secret of beauty and brilliance dwells in a proper understanding and adjustment of values, and music is powerless to help him here. Let us therefore defer the discussion of this musical parallel, which is full of pitfalls, until we have made some examination into such simple emotional reactions as color can be discovered to yield. The musical art began from the emotional response to certain simple tones and combinations, and the delight of the ear in their repetition and variation.

On account of our undeveloped sensitivity, the emotional reactions to color are found to be largely personal and whimsical: one person "loves" pink, another purple, or green. Color therapeutics is too new a thing to be relied upon for data, for even though colors are susceptible of classification as sedative, recuperative and stimulating, no two classifications arrived at independently would be likely to correspond. Most people appear to prefer bright, pure colors when presented to them in small areas, red and blue being the favourites. Certain data have been accumulated regarding the physiological effect and psychological value of different colors, but this order of research is in its infancy, and we shall have recourse, therefore, to theory, in the absence of any safer guide.

One of the theories which may be said to have justified itself in practice in a different field is that upon which is based Delsarte's famous art of expression. It has schooled some of the finest actors in the world, and raised others from mediocrity to distinction. The Delsarte system is founded upon the idea that man is a triplicity of physical, emotional, and intellectual qualities or attributes, and that the entire body and every part thereof conforms to, and expresses this triplicity. The generative and digestive region corresponds with the physical nature, the breast with the emotional, and the head with the intellectual; "below" represents the nadir of ignorance and dejection, "above" the zenith of wisdom and spiritual power. This seems a natural, and not an arbitrary classification, having interesting confirmations and correspondencies, both in the outer world of form, and in the inner world of consciousness. Moreover, it is in accord with that theosophic scheme derived from the ancient and august wisdom of the East, which longer and better than any other has withstood the obliterating action of slow time, and is even now renascent. Let us therefore attempt to classify the colors of the spectrum according to this theory, and discover if we can how nearly such a classification is conformable to reason and experience.

The red end of the spectrum, being lowest in vibratory rate, would correspond to the physical nature, proverbially more sluggish than the emotional and mental. The phrase "like a red rag to a bull," suggests a relation between the color red and the animal consciousness established by observation. The "low-brow" is the dear lover of the red necktie; the "high-brow" is he who sees violet shadows on the snow. We "see red" when we are dominated by ignoble passion. Though the color green is associated with the idea of jealousy, it is associated also with the idea of sympathy, and jealousy in the last analysis is the fear of the loss of sympathy; it belongs, at all events to the mediant, or emotional group of colors; while blue and violet are proverbially intellectual and spiritual colors, and their place in the spectrum therefore conforms to the demands of our theoretical division. Here, then, is something reasonably certain, certainly reasonable, and may serve as an hypothesis to be confirmed or confuted by subsequent research. Coming now finally to the consideration of the musical parallel, let us divide a color scale of twelve steps or semi-tones into three groups; each group, graphically portrayed, subtending one-third of the arc of a circle. The first or red group will be related to the physical nature, and will consist of purple-red, red, red-orange, and orange. The second, or green group will be related to the emotional nature, and will consist of yellow, yellow-green, green, and green-blue. The third, or blue group will be related to the intellectual and spiritual nature, and will consist of blue, blue-violet, violet and purple. The merging of purple into purple-red will then correspond to the meeting place of the highest with the lowest, "spirit" and "matter." We conceive of this meeting-place symbolically as the "heart"—the vital centre. Now "sanguine" is the appropriate name associated with the color of the blood—a color between purple and purple-red. It is logical, therefore, to regard this point in our color-scale as its tonic—"middle C"—though each color, just as in music each note, is itself the tonic of a scale of its own.

Mr. Louis Wilson—the author of the above "ophthalmic color scale" makes the same affiliation between sanguine, or blood color, and middle C, led thereto by scientific reasons entirely unassociated with symbolism. He has omitted orange-yellow and violet-purple; this makes the scale conform more exactly with the diatonic scale of two tetra-chords; it also gives a greater range of purples, a color indispensable to the artist. Moreover, in the scale as it stands, each color is exactly opposite its true spectral complementary.

The color scale being thus established and broadly divided, the next step is to find how well it justifies itself in practice. The most direct way would be to translate the musical chords recognized and dealt with in the science of harmony into their corresponding color combinations.

For the benefit of such readers as have no knowledge of musical harmony it should be said that the entire science of harmony is based upon the *triad*, or chord of three notes, and that there are various kinds of triads: the major, the minor, the augmented, the diminished, and the altered. The major triad consists of the first note of the diatonic scale, or tonic; its third, and its fifth. The minor triad differs from the major only in that the second member is lowered a semi-tone. The augmented triad differs from the major only in that the third member is raised a semi-tone. The diminished triad differs from the minor only in that the third member is lowered a semi-tone. The altered triad is a chord different by a semi-tone from any of the above.

The major triad in color is formed by taking any one of the twelve color-centers of the ophthalmic color scale as the first member of the triad; and, reading up the scale, the fifth step (each step representing a semi-tone) determines the second member, while the third member is found in the eighth step. The minor triad in color is formed by lowering the second member of the major triad one step; the augmented triad by raising the third member of the major triad one step, and the diminished triad by lowering the third member of the minor triad one step.

These various triads are shown graphically in Figure 18 as triangles within a circle divided into twelve equal parts, each part representing a semi-tone of the chromatic scale. It is seen at a glance that in every case each triad has one of its notes (an apex) in or immediately adjacent to a different one of the grand divisions of the colour scale hereinbefore established and described, and that the same thing would be true in any "key": that is, by any variation of the point of departure.

This certainly satisfies the mind in that it suggests variety in unity, balance, completeness, and in the actual portrayal, in color, of these chords in any "key" this judgment is confirmed by the eye, provided that the colors have been thrown into proper *harmonic suppression*. By this is meant such an adjustment of relative values, or such an establishment of relative proportions as will produce the maximum of beauty of which any given combination is capable. This matter imperatively demands an æsthetic sense the most sensitive.

So this "musical parallel," interesting and reasonable as it is, will not carry the color harmonist very far, and if followed too literally it is even likely to hamper him in the higher reaches of his art, for some of the musical dissonances are of great beauty in color translation. All that can safely be said in regard to the musical parallel in its present stage of development is that it simplifies and systematizes color knowledge and experiment and to a beginner it is highly educational.

If we are to have color symphonies, the best are not likely to be those based on a literal translation of some musical masterpiece into color according to this or any theory, but those created by persons who are emotionally reactive to this medium, able to imagine in color, and to treat it imaginatively. The most beautiful mobile color effects yet witnessed by the author were produced on a field only five inches square, by an eminent painter quite ignorant of music; while some of the most unimpressive have been the result of a rigid adherence to the musical parallel by persons intent on cutting, with this sword, this Gordian knot.

Into the subject of means and methods it is not proposed to enter, nor to attempt to answer such questions as to whether the light shall be direct or projected; whether the spectator, wrapped in darkness, shall watch the music unfold at the end of some mysterious vista, or whether his whole organism shall be played upon by powerful waves of multi-coloured light. These coupled alternatives are not mutually exclusive, any more than the idea of an orchestra is exclusive of that of a single human voice.

In imagining an art of mobile color unconditioned by considerations of mechanical difficulty or of expense, ideas multiply in truly bewildering profusion. Sunsets, solar coronas, star spectra, auroras such as were never seen on sea or land; rainbows, bubbles, rippling water; flaming volcanoes, lava streams of living light—these and a hundred other enthralling and perfectly realizable effects suggest themselves. What Israfil of the future will pour on mortals this new "music of the spheres"?

LOUIS SULLIVAN

PROPHET OF DEMOCRACY

Due tribute has been paid to Mr. Louis Sullivan as an architect in the first essay of this volume. That aspect of his genius has been critically dealt with by many, but as an author he is scarcely known. Yet there are Sibylline leaves of his, still let us hope in circulation, which have wielded a potent influence on the minds of a generation of men now passing to maturity. It is in the hope that his message may not be lost to the youth of today and of tomorrow that the present author now undertakes to summarize and interpret that message to a public to which Mr. Sullivan is indeed a name, but not a voice.

That he is not a voice can be attributed neither to his lack of eloquence—for he is eloquent—nor to the indifference of the younger generation of architects which has grown up since he has ceased, in any public way, to speak. It is due rather to a curious fatality whereby his memorabilia have been confined to sheets which the winds of time have scattered—pamphlets, ephemeral magazines, trade journals—never the bound volume which alone guards the sacred flame from the gusts of evil chance.

And Mr. Sullivan's is a "sacred flame," because it was kindled solely with the idea of service—a beacon to keep young men from shipwreck traversing those straits made dangerous by the Scylla of Conventionality, and the Charybdis of License. The labour his writing cost him was enormous. "I shall never again make so great a sacrifice for the younger generation," he says in a letter, "I am amazed to note how insignificant, how almost nil is the effect produced, in comparison to the cost, in vitality to me. Or perhaps it is I who am in error. Perhaps one must have reached middle age, or the Indian Summer of life, must have seen much, heard much, felt and produced much and been much in solitude to receive in reading what I gave in writing 'with hands overfull.'"

This was written with reference to *Kindergarten Chats. A sketch Analysis of Contemporaneous American Architecture*, which constitutes Mr. Sullivan's most extended and characteristic preachment to the young men of his day. It appeared in 1901, in fifty-two consecutive numbers of *The Interstate Architect and Builder*, a magazine now no longer published. In it the author, as mentor, leads an imaginary disciple up and down the land, pointing out to him the "bold, upholsterrific blunders" to be found in the architecture of the day, and commenting on them in a caustic, colloquial style—large, loose, discursive—a blend of Ruskin, Carlyle and Whitman, yet all Mr. Sullivan's own. He descends, at times, almost to ribaldry, at others he rises to poetic and prophetic heights. This is all a part of his method alternately to shame and inspire his pupil to some sort of creative activity. The syllabus of Mr. Sullivan's scheme, as it existed in his mind during the writing of *Kindergarten Chats*, and outlined by him in a letter to the author is such a torch of illumination that it is quoted here entire.

> A young man who has "finished his education" at the architectural schools comes to me for a post-graduate course—hence a free form of dialogue.
>
> I proceed with his education rather by indirection and suggestion than by direct precept. I subject him to certain experiences and allow the impressions they make on him to infiltrate, and, as I note the effect, I

gradually use a guiding hand. I supply the yeast, so to speak, and allow the ferment to work in him.

This is the gist of the whole scheme. It remains then to determine, carefully, the kind of experiences to which I shall subject the lad, and in what order, or logical (and especially psychological) sequence. I begin, then, with aspects that are literal, objective, more or less cynical, and brutal, and philistine. A little at a time I introduce the subjective, the refined, the altruistic; and, by a to-and-fro increasingly intense rhythm of these two opposing themes, worked so to speak in counterpoint, I reach a preliminary climax: of brutality tempered by a longing for nobler, purer things.

Hence arise a purblind revulsion and yearning in the lad's soul; the psychological moment has arrived, and I take him at once into the *country*—(Summer: The Storm). This is the first of the four out-of-door scenes, and the lad's first real experience with nature. It impresses him crudely but violently; and in the tense excitement of the tempest he is inspired to temporary eloquence; and at the close is much softened. He feels in a way but does not know that he has been a participant in one of Nature's superb dramas. (Thus do I insidiously prepare the way for the notion that creative architecture is in essence a dramatic art, and an art of eloquence; of subtle rhythmic beauty, power, and tenderness).

Left alone in the country the lad becomes maudlin—a callow lover of nature—and makes feeble attempts at verse. Returning to the city he melts and unbosoms—the tender shaft of the unknowable Eros has penetrated to his heart—Nature's subtle spell is on him, to disappear and reappear. Then follow discussions, more or less didactic, leading to the second out-of-door scene (Autumn Glory). Here the lad does most of the talking and shows a certain lucidity and calm of mind. The discussion of Responsibility, Democracy, Education, etc., has inevitably detached the lurking spirit of pessimism. It has to be:—Into the depths and darkness we descend, and the work reaches the tragic climax in the third out-of-door scene—Winter.

Now that the forces have been gathered and marshalled the true, sane movement of the work is entered upon and pushed at high tension, and with swift, copious modulations to its foreordained climax and optimistic peroration in the fourth and last out-of-door scene as portrayed in the Spring Song. The *locale* of this closing number is the beautiful spot in the woods, on the shore of Biloxi Bay:—where I am writing this.

I would suggest in passing that a considerable part of the K.C. is in rhythmic prose—some of it declamatory. I have endeavoured throughout this work to represent, or reproduce to the mind and heart of the reader the spoken word and intonation—not written language. It really should be read aloud, especially the descriptive and exalted passages.

There was a movement once on the part of Mr. Sullivan's admirers to issue *Kindergarten Chats* in book form, but he was asked to tone it down and expurgate it, a thing which he very naturally refused to do. Mr. Sullivan has always been completely alive to our cowardice when it comes to hearing the truth about ourselves, and alive to the danger which this cowardice entails, for to his imaginary pupil he says,

> If you wish to read the current architecture of your country, you must go at it courageously, and not pick out merely the little bits that please you. I am going to soak you with it until you are absolutely nauseated, and your faculties turn in rebellion. I may be a hard taskmaster, but I strive to be a good one. When I am through with you, you will know architecture from the ground up. You will know its virtuous reality and you will know the fake and the fraud and the humbug. I will spare nothing—for your sake. I will stir up the cesspool to its utmost depths of stench, and also the pious, hypocritical virtues of our so-called architecture—the nice, good, mealy-mouthed, suave, dexterous, diplomatic architecture, I will show you also the kind of architecture our "cultured" people believe in. And why do they believe in it? Because they do not believe in themselves.

Kindergarten Chats is even more pertinent and pointed today than it was some twenty years ago, when it was written. Speech that is full of truth is timeless, and therefore prophetic. Mr. Sullivan forecast some of the very evils by which we have been overtaken. He was able to do this on account of the fundamental soundness of his point of view, which finds expression in the following words: "Once you learn to look upon architecture not merely as an art more or less well, or more or less badly done, but as a *social manifestation*, the critical eye becomes clairvoyant, and obscure, unnoted phenomena become illumined."

Looking, from this point of view, at the office buildings that the then newly-realized possibilities of steel construction were sending skyward along lower Broadway, in New York, Mr. Sullivan reads in them a denial of democracy. To him they signify much more than they seem to, or mean to; they are more than the betrayal of architectural ignorance and mendacity, they are symptomatic of forces undermining American life.

> These buildings, as they increase in number, make this city poorer, morally and spiritually; they drag it down and down into the mire. This is not American civilization; it is the rottenness of Gomorrah. This is not Democracy—it is savagery. It shows the glutton hunt for the Dollar with no thought for aught else under the sun or over the earth. It is decadence of the spirit in its most revolting form; it is rottenness of the heart and corruption of the mind. So truly does this architecture reflect the causes which have brought it into being. Such structures are *profoundly anti-social*, and as such, they must be reckoned with. These buildings are not architecture, but outlawry, and their authors criminals in the true sense of the word. And such is the architecture of lower New York—hopeless, degraded, and putrid in its pessimistic denial of our art, and of our growing civilization—its cynical contempt for all those qualities that real humans value.

We have always been very glib about democracy; we have assumed that this country was a democracy because we named it so. But now that we are called upon to die for the idea, we find that we have never realized it anywhere except perhaps in our secret hearts. In the life of Abraham Lincoln, in the poetry of Walt Whitman, in the architecture of Louis Sullivan, the spirit of democracy found utterance, and to the extent that we ourselves partake of that spirit, it will find utterance also in us. Mr. Sullivan is a "prophet of democracy" not alone in his buildings but in his writings, and the prophetic note is sounded even more clearly in his *What is Architecture? A Study in the American People of Today*, than in *Kindergarten Chats*.

This essay was first printed in *The American Contractor* of January 6, 1906, and afterwards issued in brochure form. The author starts by tracing architecture to its root in the human mind: this physical thing is the manifestation of a psychological state. As a man thinks, so he is; he acts according to his thought, and if that act takes the form of a building it is an emanation of his inmost life, and reveals it.

> Everything is there for us to read, to interpret; and this we may do at our leisure. The building has not means of locomotion, it cannot hide itself, it cannot get away. There it is, and there it will stay—telling more truths about him who made it, than he in his fatuity imagines; revealing his mind and his heart exactly for what they are worth, not a whit more, not a whit less; telling plainly the lies he thinks; telling with almost cruel truthfulness his bad faith, his feeble, wabbly mind, his impudence, his selfish egoism, his mental irresponsibility, his apathy, his disdain for real things—until at last the building says to us: "I am no more a real building than the thing that made me is a real man!"

Language like this stings and burns, but it is just such as is needful to shame us out of our comfortable apathy, to arouse us to new responsibilities, new opportunities. Mr. Sullivan, awake among the sleepers, drenches us with bucketfuls of cold, tonic, energizing truth. The poppy and mandragora of the past, of Europe, poisons us, but in this, our hour of battle, we must not be permitted to dream on. He saw, from far back, that "we, as a people, not only have betrayed each other, but have failed in that trust which the world spirit of democracy placed in our hands, as we, a new people, emerged to fill a new and spacious land." It has taken a world war to make us see the situation as he saw it, and it is to us, a militant nation, and not to the slothful civilians a decade ago, that Mr. Sullivan's stirring message seems to be addressed.

The following quotation is his first crack of the whip at the architectural schools. The problem of education is to him of all things the most vital; in this essay he returns to it again and again, while of *Kindergarten Chats* it is the very *raison d'être*.

> I trust that a long disquisition is not necessary in order to show that the attempt at imitation, by us, of this day, of the by-gone forms of building, is a procedure unworthy of a free people; and that the dictum of the schools, that Architecture is finished and done, is a suggestion humiliating to every active brain, and therefore, in fact, a puerility and a falsehood when weighed in the scales of truly democratic thought. Such dictum gives the lie in arrogant fashion, to healthful human experience. It says, in a word: the American people are not fit for democracy.

He finds the schools saturated with superstitions which are the survivals of the scholasticism of past centuries—feudal institutions, in effect, inimical to his idea of the true spirit of democratic education. This he conceives of as a searching-out, liberating, and developing the splendid but obscured powers of the average man, and particularly those of children. "It is disquieting to note," he says, "that the system of education on which we lavish funds with such generous, even prodigal, hand, falls short of fulfilling its true democratic function; and that particularly in the so-called higher branches its tendency appears daily more reactionary, more feudal. It is not an agreeable reflection that so many of our university graduates lack the trained ability to see clearly, and to think clearly, concisely, constructively; that there is perhaps more showing of cynicism than good faith, seemingly more distrust of men than confidence in them, and, withal, no consummate ability to interpret things."

In contrast to the schoolman he sketches the psychology of the active-minded but "uneducated" man, with sympathy and understanding, the man who is courageously seeking a way with little to guide and help him.

> Is it not the part of wisdom to cheer, to encourage such a mind, rather than dishearten it with ridicule? To say to it: Learn that the mind works best when allowed to work naturally; learn to do what your problem suggests when you have reduced it to its simplest terms; you will thus find that all problems, however complex, take on a simplicity you had not dreamed of; accept this simplicity boldly, and with confidence, do not lose your nerve and run away from it, or you are lost, for you are here at the point men so heedlessly call genius—as though it were necessarily rare; for you are here at the point no living brain can surpass in essence, the point all truly great minds seek—the point of vital simplicity—the point of view which so illuminates the mind that the art of expression becomes spontaneous, powerful, and unerring, and achievement a certainty. So, if you seek and express the best that is in yourself, you must search out the best that is in your people; for they are your problem, and you are indissolubly a part of them. It is for you to affirm that which they really wish to affirm, namely, the best that is in them, and they as truly wish you to express the best that is in yourself. If the people seem to have but little faith it is because they have been tricked so long; they are weary of dishonesty, more weary than they know, much more weary than you know, and in their hearts they seek honest and fearless men, men simple and clear in mind, loyal to their own manhood and to the people. The American people are now in a stupor; be on hand at the awakening.

Next he pays his respects to current architectural criticism—a straining at gnats and a swallowing of camels, by minds "benumbed by culture," and hearts made faint by the tyranny of precedent. He complains that they make no distinction between *was* and *is*, too readily assuming that all that is left us moderns is the humble privilege to select, copy and adapt.

> The current mannerisms of Architectural criticism must often seem trivial. For of what avail is it to say that this is too small, that too large, this too thick, and that too thin, or to quote this, that, or the other precedent, when the real question may be: Is not the entire design a mean evasion? Why magnify this, that, or the other little thing, if the entire scheme of thinking that the building stands for is false, and puts a mask upon the people, who want true buildings, but do not know how to get them so long as Architects betray them with Architectural phrases?

And so he goes on with his Jeremiad: a prophet of despair, do you say? No, he seeks to destroy only that falsity which would confine the living spirit. Earlier and more clearly than we, he discerned the menace to our civilization of the unrestricted play of the masculine forces—powerful, ruthless, disintegrating—the head dominating the heart. It has taken the surgery of war to open our eyes, and behold the spectacle of the entire German nation which by an intellectual process appears to have killed out compassion, enthroning *Schrecklichkeit*. In the heart alone dwells hope of salvation. "For he who knows even a genuinely little of Mankind knows this truth: the heart is greater than the head. For in the heart is Desire; and from it come forth Courage and Magnanimity."

> You have not thought deeply enough to know that the heart in you is the woman in man. You have derided your femininity, where you have suspected it; whereas, you should have known its power, cherished and utilized it, for it is the hidden well-spring of Intuition and Imagination. What can the brain accomplish without these two? They are the man's two inner eyes; without them he is stone blind. For the mind sets forth their powers both together. One carries the light, the other searches; and between them they find treasures. These they bring to the brain, which first elaborates them, then says to the will, "Do"—and Action follows. Poetically considered, as far as the huge, disordered resultant mass of your Architecture is concerned, Intuition and Imagination have not gone forth to illuminate and search the hearts of the people. Thus are its works stone blind.

It is the absence of poetry and beauty which makes our architecture so depressing to the spirits. "Poetry as a living thing," says Mr. Sullivan, "stands for the most telling quality that a man can impart to his thoughts. Judged by this test your buildings are dreary, empty places." Artists in words, like Lafcadio Hearn and Henry James, are able to make articulate the sadness which our cities inspire, but it is a blight which lies heavy on us all. Theodore Dreiser says, in *Sister Carrie*—a book with so much bitter truth in it that it was suppressed by the original publishers:

> Once the bright days of summer pass by, a city takes on the sombre garb of grey, wrapped in which it goes about its labors during the long winter. Its endless buildings look grey, its sky and its streets assume a sombre hue; the scattered, leafless trees and wind-blown dust and paper but add to the general solemnity of color. There seems to be something in the chill breezes which scurry through the long, narrow thoroughfares productive of rueful thoughts. Not poets alone, nor artists, nor that superior order of mind which arrogates to itself all refinement, feel this, but dogs and all men.

The excuse that we are too young a people to have developed an architecture instinct with that natural poetry which so charms us in the art of other countries and other times, Mr. Sullivan disposes of in characteristic fashion. To the plea that "We are too young to consider these accomplishments. We have been so busy with our material development that we have not found time to consider them," he makes answer as follows:

> Know, then, to begin with, they are not accomplishments but necessaries. And, to end with, you are old enough, and have found the time to succeed

in nearly making a fine art of—Betrayal, and a science of—Graft. Know that you are as old as the race. That each man among you had in him the accumulated power of the race, ready at hand for use, in the right way, when he shall conclude it better to think straight and hence act straight rather than, as now, to act crooked and pretend to be straight. Know that the test, plain, simple *honesty* (and you all know, every man of you knows, exactly what that means) is always at your hand.

Know that as all complex manifestations have a simple basis of origin, so the vast complexity of your national unrest, ill health, inability to think clearly and accurately concerning simple things, really vital things, is easily traceable to the single, actual, active cause—Dishonesty; and that this points with unescapable logic and in just measure to each individual man!

The remedy;—*individual honesty*.

To the objection that this is too simple a solution, Mr. Sullivan retorts that all great solutions are simple, that the basic things of the universe are those which the heart of a child might comprehend. "Honesty stands in the universe of Human Thought and Action, as its very Centre of Gravity, and is our human mask-word behind which abides all the power of Nature's Integrity, the profoundest *fact* which modern thinking has persuaded Life to reveal."

If, on the other hand, the reader complains, "All this is above our heads," Mr. Sullivan is equally ready with an answer:

No, it is not. *It is close beside your hand!* and therein
    lies its power.

Again you say, "How can honesty be enforced?"

It cannot be enforced!

"Then how will the remedy go into effect?"

It cannot *go* into effect. It can only come into effect.

"Then how can it come?"

Ask Nature.

"And what will Nature say?"

> Nature is always saying: "I centre at each man, woman and child. I knock at the door of each heart, and I wait. I wait in patience—ready to enter with my gifts."

"And is that all that Nature says?"

That is all.

"Then how shall we receive Nature?"

> By opening wide your minds! For your greatest crime against yourselves is that you have locked the door and thrown away the key!

Thus, by a long detour, Mr. Sullivan returns to his initial proposition, that the falsity of our architecture can be corrected only by integrity of thought. "Thought is the fine and powerful instrument. Therefore, *have thought for the integrity of your own thought.*"

> Naturally, then, as your thoughts thus change, your growing architecture will change. Its falsity will depart; its reality will gradually appear. For the integrity of your thought as a People, will then have penetrated the minds of your architects.

> Then, too, *as your basic thought changes, will emerge a philosophy, a poetry, and an art of expression in all things; for you will have learned that a characteristic philosophy, poetry and art of expression are vital to the healthful growth and development of a democratic people.*

Some readers may complain that these are after all only glittering generalities, of no practical use in solving the specific problems with which every architect is confronted. On the contrary they are fundamental verities of incalculable benefit to every sincere artist. Shallowness is the great vice of democracy; it is surface without depth, a welter of concrete detail in which the mind easily loses those great, underlying abstractions from which alone great art can spring. These, in this essay, Mr. Sullivan helps us to recapture, and inspires us to employ. He would win us from our insincerities, our trivialities, and awaken our enormous latent, unused power. He says:

Awaken it.

Use it.

Use it for the common good.

Begin now!

> For it is as true today as when one of your wise men said it:—

"The way to resume is to resume!"

COLOR AND CERAMICS

The production of ceramics—perhaps the oldest of all the useful arts practised by man; an art with a magnificent history—seems to be entering upon a new era of development. It is more alive today, more generally, more skilfully, though not more *artfully* practised than ever before. It should therefore be of interest to all lovers of architecture, in view of the increasing importance of ceramics in building, to consider the ways in which these materials may best be used.

Looking at the matter in the broadest possible way, it may be said that the building impulse throughout the ages has expressed itself in two fundamentally different types of structure: that in which the architecture—and even the ornament—is one with the engineering; and that in which the two elements are separable, not in thought alone, but in fact. For brevity let us name that manner of building in which the architecture is the construction, *Inherent* architecture, and that manner in which the two are separable *Incrusted* architecture.

To the first class belong the architectures of Egypt, Greece, and Gothic architecture as practised in the north of Europe; to the second belong Roman architecture of the splendid period, Moorish architecture, and Italian Gothic, so called. In the first class the bones of the building were also its flesh; in the second bones and flesh were in a manner separable, as is proven by the fact that they were separately considered, separately fashioned. Ruined Karnak, the ruined Parthenon, wrecked Rheims, show ornament so integral a part of the fabric—etched so deep—that what has survived of the one has survived also of the other; while the ruined Baths of Caracalla the uncompleted church of S. Petronio in Bologna, and many a stark mosque on many a sandy desert show only bare skeletons of whose completed glory we can only guess. In them the fabric was a framework for the display of the lapidary or the ceramic art—a garment destroyed, rent, or tattered by time and chance, leaving the bones still strong, but bare.

This classification of architecture into Inherent and Incrusted is not to be confused with the discrimination between architecture that is *Arranged*, and architecture that is *Organic*, a classification which is based on psychology—like the difference between the business man and the poet: talent and genius—whereas the classification which the reader is asked now to consider is based rather on the matter of expediency in the use of materials. Let us draw no invidious comparisons between Inherent and Incrusted architecture, but regard each as the adequate expression of an ideal type of beauty; the one masculine, since in the male figure the osseous framework is more easily discernible; the other feminine, because more concealed and overlaid with a cellular tissue of shining, precious materials, on which the disruptive forces in man and nature are more free to act.

It is scarcely necessary to state that it is with Incrusted architecture that we are alone concerned in this discussion, for to this class almost all modern buildings perforce belong. This is by reason of a necessity dictated by the materials that we employ, and by our methods of construction. All modern buildings follow practically one method of construction: a bony framework of steel—or of concrete reinforced by steel—filled in and subdivided by concrete, brick, hollow fire-clay, or some of its substitutes. To a construction of this kind some sort of an outer encasement is not only æsthetically desirable, but practically necessary. It usually takes the form of stone, face-brick, terra-cotta, tile, stucco, or some combination of two or more of these materials. Of the two types of architecture the Incrusted type is therefore imposed by structural necessity.

The enormous importance of ceramics in its relation to architecture thus becomes apparent. They minister to an architectural need instead of gratifying an architectural whim. Ours is a period of Incrusted architecture—one which demands the encasement, rather than the exposure of structure, and therefore logically admits of the enrichment of surfaces by means of "veneers" of materials more precious and beautiful than those employed in the structure, which becomes, as it were, the canvas of the picture, and not the picture itself. For these purposes there are no materials more apt, more adaptable, more enduring, richer in potentialities of beauty than the products of ceramic art. They are easily and inexpensively produced of any desired shape, color, texture; their hard, dense surface resists the action of the elements, is not easily soiled, and is readily cleaned; being fashioned by fire they are fire resistant.

So much then for the practical demands, in modern architecture, met by the products of ceramic art. The æsthetic demand is not less admirably met—or rather *might* be.

When, in the sixteenth century, the Renaissance spread from south to north, color was practically eliminated from architecture. The Egyptians had had it, hot and bright as the sun on the desert; we know that the Greeks made their Parian marble glow in rainbow tints; Moorish architecture was nothing if not colorful, and the Venice Ruskin loved was fairly iridescent—a thing of fire-opal and pearl. In Italian Renaissance architecture up to its latest phase, the color element was always present; but it was snuffed out under the leaden colored northern skies. Paris is grey, London is brown, New York is white, and Chicago the color of cinders. We have only to compare them to yellow Rome, red Siena, and pearl-tinted Venice, to realize how much we have lost in the elimination of color from architecture. We are coming to realize it. Color played an important part in the Pan-American Exposition, and again in the San Francisco Exposition, where, wedded to light, it became the dominant note of the whole architectural concert. Now these great expositions in which the architects and artists are given a free hand, are in the nature of preliminary studies in which these functionaries sketch in transitory form the things they desire to do in more permanent form. They are forecasts of the future, a future which in certain quarters is already beginning to realize itself. It is therefore probable that architectural art will become increasingly colorful.

The author remembers the day and the hour when this became his personal conviction—his personal desire. It happened years ago in the Albright Gallery in Buffalo—a building then newly completed, of a severely classic type. In the central hall was a single doorway, whose white marble architrave had been stained with different colored pigments by Francis Bacon; after the manner of the Greeks. The effect was so charming, and made the rest of the place seem by contrast so cold and dun, that the author came then and there to the conclusion that architecture without polychromy was architecture incomplete. Mr. Bacon spent three years in Asia Minor, and elsewhere, studying the remains of Greek architecture, and he found and brought home a fragment of an antefix from the temple of Assos, in which the applied color was still pure and strong. The Greeks were a joyous people. When joy comes back into life, color will come back into architecture.

Ceramic products are ideal as a means to this end. The Greeks themselves recognized their value for they used them widely and wisely: it has been discovered that they even attached bands of colored terra-cotta to the marble mouldings of their temples. How different must have been such a temple's real appearance from that imagined by the Classical Revivalists, whose tradition of the inviolable cold Parian purity of Greek architecture has persisted, even against archæological evidence to the contrary, up to the present day.

In one way we have an advantage over the Greek, if we only had the wit to profit by it. His palette, like his musical scale, was more limited than ours. Nearly the whole gamut of the spectrum is now available to the architect who wishes to employ ceramics. The colors do not change or fade, and possess a beautiful quality. Our craftsmen and manufacturers of face-brick, terra-cotta, and colored tile, after much costly experimentation, have succeeded in producing ceramics of a high order of excellence and intrinsic beauty; they can do practically anything demanded of them; but from that quarter where they should reap the greatest commercial advantage—the field of architecture—there is all too little demand. The architect who should lead, teach and dictate in this field, is often through ignorance obliged to learn and follow instead. This has led to an ignominious situation—ignominious, that is, to the architect. He has come to require of the manufacturer—when he requires anything at all—assistance in the very matter in which he should assist: the determination of color design. It is no wonder that the results are often bad, and therefore discouraging. The manufacturers of ceramics welcome co-operation and assistance on the part of the architect with an eagerness which is almost pathetic, on those rare occasions when assistance is offered.

But the architect is not really to blame: the reason for his failure lies deep in his general predicament of having to know a little of everything, and do a great deal more than he can possibly do well. To cope with this, if his practice warrants the expenditure, he surrounds himself with specialists in various fields, and assigns various departments of his work to them. He cannot be expected to have on his staff a specialist in ceramics, nor can he, with all his manifold activities, be expected to become such a specialist himself. As a result, he is usually content to let color problems alone, for they are just another complication of his already too complicated life; or he refers them to some one whom he thinks ought to know—a manufacturer's designer—and approves almost anything submitted. Of course the ideal architect would have time for every problem, and solve it supremely well; but the real architect is all too human: there are depressions on his cranium where bumps ought to be; moreover, he wants a little time left to energize in other directions than in the practice of his craft. One of the functions of architecture is to reveal the inherent qualities and beauties of different materials, by their appropriate use and tasteful display. An onyx staircase on the one hand, and a portland cement high altar on the other, alike violate this function of architecture; they transgress that beautiful necessity which decrees that precious materials should serve precious uses and common materials should serve utilitarian ends. Now color is a precious thing, and its highest beauties can be brought out only by contrast with broad neutral tinted spaces. The interior walls of a mediaeval cathedral never competed with its windows, and by the same token, a riot of polychromy all over the side of a building is not as effective, even from a chromatic point of view, as though it were confined, say, to an entrance and a frieze. Gilbert's witty phrase is applicable here:

"Where everybody's somebody, nobody's anybody."

Let us build our walls, then, of stone, or brick, or stucco,—for their flat surfaces and neutral tints conduce to that repose so essential to good architectural effect: but let us not rest content with this, but grant to the eye the delight and contentment which it craves, by color and pattern placed at those points to which it is desirable to attract attention, for they serve the same æsthetic purpose as a tiara on the brow of beauty, or a ring on a delicate white hand. But just as jewelry is best when it is most individual, so the ornament of a building should be in keeping with its general character and complexion. A color scheme should not be chosen at random, but dictated by the prevailing tone and texture of the wall surfaces, with which it should harmonize as inevitably as the blossom of a bush with its prevailing tone of stems and foliage. In a building this prevailing tone will inevitably be either cold or warm, and the color scheme just as inevitably should be either cold or warm; that is, there should be a preponderance of cold colors over warm, or vice versa. Otherwise the eye will suffer just that order of uneasiness which comes from the contemplation of two equal masses, whereas it experiences satisfaction in proportionate unequals.

Nothing will take the place of an instinctive colour-sense, but even that needs the training of experience, if the field be new, and a few general principles of all but universal application will not be amiss.

First of all it should be remembered that the intensity of color should be carefully adjusted to its area. It is dangerous to try to use high, pure colors, unrelieved and uncontrasted, in large masses, but the brightest, strongest colors may be used with safety in units of sufficiently restricted size. For harmony, as well as for richness, the law of complementaries, in its most general application, is the safest of all guides, but it must be followed with fine discrimination. Complementary colors are like married pairs, if they find the right adjustment with one another they are happy—that is, there is an effect of beauty—but lacking such adjustment they are worse off together than apart. Every artist who experiments in color soon finds out for himself that instead of using two colors directly complementary, it is better to "split" one of them, that is, use instead of one of them two others, which combined will yield the color in question. For example, the color complementary to red is green-blue. Now green-blue is equidistant between yellow-green and blue-violet, so if for red and blue-green; red, yellow-green and blue-violet be substituted the combination loses its obviousness and a certain harshness without losing anything of its brilliance, or without departing from the optical law involved. Such a combination corresponds to a diminished triad in music.

Another important consideration with regard to color as employed by the architect dwells in those optical changes effected by distance and position: the relative visibility of different colors and combinations of colors as the spectator recedes from them, and the environmental changes which colors undergo—in bright sunlight, in shadow, against the sky, and with relation to backgrounds of different sorts.

The effect of distance is to make colors merge into one another, to lower the values, but not all equally. Yellow loses itself first, tending toward white. The effect of distance, in general, is to disintegrate and decompose, thus giving "vibration" as it is called. A knowledge of these and kindred facts will save the architect from many disappointments and enable him to obtain wonderful chromatic effects by simple means.

Many architects unused to color problems design their ornament with very little thought about the colors which they propose to employ, making it an after-consideration; but the two things should be considered synchronously for the best final effect. There is a cryptic saying that "color is at right angles to form," that is, color is capable of making surfaces advance toward or recede from the eye, just as modelling does; and for this reason, if color is used, a great deal of modelling may be dispensed with. If a receding color is used on a recessed plane, it deepens that plane unduly; while on the other hand if a color which refuses to recede—like yellow for example—is used where depth is wanted, the receding plane and the approaching color neutralize one another, resulting in an effect of flatness not intended. The tyro should not complicate his problem by combining color with high relief modelling, bringing inevitably in the element of light and shade. He should leave that for older hands and concern himself rather with flat or nearly flat surfaces, using his modelling much as the worker in cloisonné uses his little rims of brass—to confine and define each color within its own allotted area. Then, as he gains experience, he may gradually enrich his pattern by the addition of the element of light and shade, should he so decide.

Now as to certain general considerations in relation to the appropriate and logical use of ceramics in the construction and adornment of buildings, exterior and interior. In our northern latitudes care should be taken that ceramics are not used in places and in ways where the accumulation of snow and ice render the joints subject to alternate freezing and thawing, for in such case, unless the joints are protected with metal, the units will work loose in time. On vertical surfaces such protection is not necessary; the use of ceramics should therefore be confined for the most part to such surfaces: for friezes, panels, door and window architraves, and the like. When it is desirable for æsthetic reasons to tie a series of windows together vertically by means of some "fill" of a material different from that of the body of the wall, ceramics lend themselves admirably to the purpose—better than wood, which rots; than iron, which rusts; than bronze, which turns black; and than marble, which soon loses its color and texture in exposed situations of this sort.

On the interior of buildings, the most universal use of ceramics is, of course, for floors, and with the non-slip devices of various sorts which have come into the market, they are no less good for stairs. There is nothing better for wainscoting, and in fact for any surface whatsoever subject to soil and wear. These materials combine permanent protection and permanent decoration. But fired by the zeal of the convert the use of ceramics may be overdone. One easily recalls entire rooms of this material, floors, walls, ceilings, which are less successful than as though a variety of materials had been employed. It is just such variety—each material treated in a characteristic, and therefore different way—that gives charm to so many foreign churches and cathedrals: walls of stone, floors of marble, choir-stalls of carved wood, and rood-screen of metal: it is the difference between an orchestra of various instruments and a mandolin orchestra or a saxaphone sextette. Ceramics should never invade the domain of the plasterer, the mural painter, the cabinet maker. Do not let us, in our zeal for ceramics, be like Bottom the weaver, eager to play every part.

Ceramics have, as regards architecture, a distinct and honorable function. This function should be recognized, taken advantage of, but never overpassed. They offer opportunities large but not limitless. They constitute one instrument of the orchestra of which the architect is the conductor, an instrument beautiful in the hands of a master, and doubly beautiful in concert and contrast with those other materials whose harmonious ensemble makes that music in three dimensions: architectural art.

SYMBOLS AND SACRAMENTS

Architecture is the concrete presentment in space of the soul of a people. If that soul be petty and sordid—"stirred like a child by little things"—no great architecture is possible because great architecture can image only greatness. Before any worthy architecture can arise in the modern world the soul must be aroused. The cannons of Europe are bringing about this awakening. The world—the world of thought and emotion from whence flow acts and events—is no longer decrepit, but like Swedenborg's angels it is advancing toward the springtide of its youth: down the ringing grooves of change "we sweep into the younger day."

After the war we are likely to witness an art evolution which will not be restricted to statues and pictures and insincere essays in dry-as-dust architectural styles, but one which will permeate the whole social fabric, and make it palpitate with the rhythm of a younger, a more abundant life. Beauty and mystery will again make their dwelling among men; the Voiceless will speak in music, and the Formless will spin rhythmic patterns on the loom of space. We shall seek and find a new language of symbols to express the joy of the soul, freed from the thrall of an iron age of materialism, and fronting the unimaginable splendors of the spiritual life.

For every æsthetic awakening is the result of a spiritual awakening of some sort. Every great religious movement found an art expression eloquent of it. When religion languished, such things as Versailles and the Paris Opera House were possible, but not such things as the Parthenon, or Notre Dame. The temples of Egypt were built for the celebration of the rites of the religion of Egypt; so also in the case of Greece. Roman architecture was more widely secular, but Rome's noblest monument, the Pantheon, was a religious edifice. The Moors, inflamed with religious ardor, swept across Europe, blazing their trail with mosques and palaces conceived seemingly in some ecstatic state of dream. The Renaissance, tainted though it was by worldliness, found still its inspiration in sacred themes, and recorded its beginning and its end in two mighty religious monuments: Brunelleschi's and Michael Angelo's domical churches, "wrought in a sad sincerity" by deeply religious men. Gothic art is a synonym for mediaeval Christianity; while in the Orient art is scarcely secular at all, but a symbolical language framed and employed for the expression of spiritual ideas.

This law, that spirituality and not materialism distils the precious attar of great art, is permanently true and perennially applicable, for laws of this order do not change from age to age, however various their manifestation. The inference is plain: until we become a religious people great architecture is far from us. We are becoming religious in that broad sense in which churches and creeds, forms and ceremonies, play little part. Ours is the search of the heart for something greater than itself which is still itself; it is the religion of brotherhood, whose creed is love, whose ritual is service.

This transformed and transforming religion of the West, the tardy fruit of the teachings of Christ, now secretly active in the hearts of men, will receive enrichment from many sources. Science will reveal the manner in which the spirit weaves its seven-fold veil of illusion; nature, freshly sensed, will yield new symbols which art will organize into a language; out of the experience of the soul will grow new rituals and observances. But one precious tincture of this new religion our civilization and our past cannot supply; it is the heritage of Asia, cherished in her brooding bosom for uncounted centuries, until, by the operation of the law of cycles, the time should come for the giving of it to the West.

This secret is Yoga, the method of self-development whereby the seeker for union is enabled to perceive the shining of the Inward Light. This is achieved by daily discipline in stilling the mind and directing the consciousness inward instead of outward. The Self is within, and the mind, which is normally centrifugal, must first be arrested, controlled, and then turned back upon itself, and held with perfect steadiness. All this is naively expressed in the Upanishads in the passage, "The Self-existent pierced the openings of the senses so that they turn forward, not backward into himself. Some wise man, however, with eyes closed and wishing for immortality, saw the Self behind." This stilling of the mind, its subjugation and control whereby it may be concentrated on anything at will, is particularly hard for persons of our race and training, a race the natural direction of whose consciousness is strongly outward, a training in which the practice of introspective meditation finds no place.

Yoga—that "union" which brings inward vision, the contribution of the East to the spiritual life of the West—will bring profound changes into the art of the West, since art springs from consciousness. The consciousness of the West now concerns itself with the visible world almost exclusively, and Western art is therefore characterized by an almost slavish fidelity to the ephemeral appearances of things—the record of particular moods and moments. The consciousness of the East on the other hand, is subjective, introspective. Its art accordingly concerns itself with eternal aspects, with a world of archetypal ideas in which things exist not for their own sake, but as symbols of supernal things. The Oriental artist avoids as far as possible trivial and individual rhythms, seeking always the fundamental rhythm of the larger, deeper life.

Now this quality so earnestly sought and so highly prized in Oriental art, is the very thing which our art and our architecture most conspicuously lack. To the eye sensitive to rhythm, our essays in these fields appear awkward and unconvincing, lacking a certain *inevitability*. We must restore to art that first great canon of Chinese æsthetics, "*Rhythmic vitality,* or the life movement of the spirit through the rhythm of things." It cannot be interjected from the outside, but must be inwardly realized by the "stilling" of the mind above described.

Art cannot dispense with symbolism; as the letters on this page convey thoughts to the mind, so do the things of this world, organized into a language of symbols, speak to the soul through art. But in the building of our towers of Babel, again mankind is stricken with a confusion of tongues. Art has no *common language;* its symbols are no longer valid, or are no longer understood. This is a condition for which materialism has no remedy, for the reason that materialism sees always the pattern but never that which the pattern represents. We must become *spiritually illumined* before we can read nature truly, and re-create, from such a reading, fresh and universal symbols for art. This is a task beyond the power of our sad generation, enchained by negative thinking, overshadowed by war, but we can at least glimpse the nature of the reaction between the mystic consciousness and the things of this world which will produce a new language of symbols. The mystic consciousness looks upon nature as an arras embroidered over with symbols of the things it conceals from view. We are ourselves symbols, dwelling in a world of symbols—a world many times removed from that ultimate reality to which all things bear figurative witness; the commonest thing has yet some mystic meaning, and ugliness and vulgarity exist only in the unillumined mind.

What mystic meaning, it may be asked, is contained in such things as a brick, a house, a hat, a pair of shoes? A brick is the ultimate atom of a building; a house is the larger body which man makes for his uses, just as the Self has built its habitation of flesh and bones; hat and shoes are felt and leather insulators with which we seek to cut ourselves off from the currents which flow through earth and air from God. It may be objected that these answers only substitute for the lesser symbol a greater, but this is inevitable: if for the greater symbol were named one still more abstract and inclusive, the ultimate verity would be as far from affirmation as before. There is nothing of which the human mind can conceive that is not a symbol of something greater and higher than itself.

The dictionary defines a symbol as "something that stands for something else and serves to represent it, or to bring to mind one or more of its qualities." Now this world is a *reflection* of a higher world, and that of a higher world still, and so on. Accordingly, everything is a symbol of something higher, since by reflecting, it "stands for, and serves to represent it," and the thing symbolized, being itself a reflection, is, by the same token, itself a symbol. By reiterated repetitions of this reflecting process throughout the numberless planes and sub-planes of nature, each thing becomes a symbol, not of one thing only, but of many things, all intimately correlated, and this gives rise to those underlying analogies, those "secret subterranean passages between matter and soul" which have ever been the especial preoccupation of the poet and the mystic, but which may one day become the subject of serious examination by scientific men.

Let us briefly pass in review the various terms of such an ascending series of symbols: members of one family, they might be called, since they follow a single line of descent.

Take gold: as a thing in itself, without any symbolical significance, it is a metallic element, having a characteristic yellow color, very heavy, very soft, the most ductile, malleable, and indestructible of metals. In its minted form it is the life force of the body economic, since on its abundance and free circulation the well-being of that body depends; it is that for which all men strive and contend, because without it they cannot comfortably live. This, then, is gold in its first and lowest symbolical aspect: a life principle, a motive force in human affairs. But it is not gold which has gained for man his lordship over nature; it is fire, the yellow gold, not of the earth, but of the air,—cities and civilizations, arts and industries, have ever followed the camp fire of the pioneer. Sunlight comes next in sequence—sunlight, which focussed in a burning glass, spontaneously produces flame. The world subsists on sunlight; all animate creation grows by it, and languishes without it, as the prosperity of cities waxes or wanes with the presence or absence of a supply of gold. The magnetic force of the sun, specialized as *prana* (which is not the breath which goes up and the breath which goes down, but that other, in which the two repose), fulfils the same function in the human body as does gold in civilization, sunlight in nature: its abundance makes for health, its meagreness for enervation. Higher than *prana* is the mind, that golden sceptre of man's dominion, the Promethean gift of fire with which he menaces the empire of the gods. Higher still, in the soul, love is the motive force, the conqueror: a "heart of gold" is one warmed and lighted by love. Still other is the desire of the spirit, which no human affection satisfies, but truth only, the Golden Person, the Light of the World, the very Godhead itself. Thus there is earthy, airy, etheric gold; gold as intellect, gold as love, gold as truth; from the curse of the world, the cause of a thousand crimes, there ascends a Jacob's Ladder of symbols to divinity itself, whereby men may learn that God works by sacrifice: that His universe is itself His broken body. As gold in the purse, fire on the forge, sunlight for the eyes, breath in the body, knowledge in the mind, love in the heart, and wisdom in the understanding, He draws all men unto Him, teaching them the wise use of wealth, the mastery over nature, the care of the body, the cultivation of the mind, the love of wife and child and neighbour, and, last lesson of all, He teaches them that in industry, in science, in art, in sympathy and understanding, He it is they are all the while knowing, loving, becoming; and that even when they flee Him, His are the wings—

"When me they fly, I am the wings."

This attempt to define gold as a symbol ends with the indication of an ubiquitous and immanent divinity in everything. Thus it is always: in attempting to dislodge a single voussoir from the arch of truth, the temple itself is shaken, so cunningly are the stones fitted together. All roads lead to Rome, and every symbol is a key to the Great Mystery: for example, read in the light of these correspondences, the alchemist's transmutation of base metals into gold, is seen to be the sublimation of man's lower nature into "that highest golden sheath, which is Brahman."

Keeping the first sequence clearly in mind, let us now attempt to trace another, parallel to it: the feminine of which the first may be considered the corresponding masculine. Silver is a white, ductile metallic element. In coinage it is the synonym for ready cash,—gold in the bank is silver in the pocket; hence, in a sense, silver is the *reflection*, or the second power of gold. Just as ruddy gold is correlated with fire, so is pale silver with water; and as fire is affiliated with the sun, so do the waters of the earth follow the moon in her courses. The golden sun, the silver moon: these commonly employed descriptive adjectives themselves supply the correlation we are seeking; another indication of its validity lies in the fact that one of the characteristics of water is its power of reflecting; that moonlight is reflected sunlight. If gold is the mind, silver is the body, in which the mind is imaged, objectified; if gold is flamelike love, silver is brooding affection; and in the highest regions of consciousness, beauty is the feminine or form side of truth—its silver mirror.

There are two forces in the world, one of projection, the other of recall; two states, activity and rest. Nature, with tireless ingenuity, everywhere publishes this fact: in bursting bud and falling seed, in the updrawn waters and the descending rain; throw a stone into the air, and when the impulse is exhausted, gravity brings it to earth again. In civilized society these centrifugal and centripetal forces find expression in the anarchic and radical spirit which breaks down and re-forms existing institutions, and in the conservative spirit which preserves and upbuilds by gradual accretion; they are analogous to igneous and to aqueous action in the formation and upbuilding of the earth itself, and find their prototype again in man and woman: man, the warrior, who prevails by the active exercise of his powers, and woman, "the treasury of the continued race," who conquers by continual quietness. Man and woman symbolize forces centrifugal and centripetal not alone in their inner nature, and in the social and economic functions peculiar to each, but in their physical aspects and peculiarities as well, for man is small of flank and broad of shoulder, with relatively large extremities, *i.e., centrifugal*: while woman is formed with broad hips, narrow shoulders, and small feet and hands, *i.e., centripetal*. Woman's instinctive and unconscious gestures are *towards* herself, man's are *away from* himself. The physiologist might hold that the anatomical differences between the sexes result from their difference in function in the reproduction and conservation of the race, and this is a true view, but the lesser truth need not necessarily exclude the greater. As Chesterton says, "Something in the evil spirit of our time forces people always to pretend to have found some material and mechanical explanation." Such would have us believe, with Schopenhauer and Bernard Shaw, that the lover's delight in the beauty of his mistress dwells solely in his instinctive perception of her fitness to be the mother of his child. This is undoubtedly a factor in the glamour woman casts on man, but there are other factors too, higher as well as lower, corresponding to different departments of our manifold nature. First of all, there is mere physical attraction: to the man physical, woman is a cup of delight; next, there is emotional love, whereby woman appeals through her need of protection, her power of tenderness; on the mental plane she is man's intellectual companion, his masculine reason would supplement itself with her feminine intuition; he recognizes in her an objectification, in some sort, of his own soul, his spirit's bride, predestined throughout the ages; while the god within him perceives her to be that portion of himself which he put forth before the world was, to be the mother, not alone of human children, but of all those myriad forms, within which entering, "as in a sheath, a knife," he becomes the Enjoyer, and realizes, vividly and concretely, his bliss, his wisdom, and his power.

Adam and Eve, and the tree in the midst of the garden! After man and woman, a tree is perhaps the most significant symbol in the world: every tree is the Tree of Life in the sense that it is a representation of universal becoming. To say that all things have for their mother *prakriti*, undifferentiated substance, and for their father *purusha*, the creative fire, is vague and metaphysical, and conveys little meaning to our image-bred, image-fed minds; on the physical plane we can only learn these transcendental truths by means of symbols, and so to each of us is given a human father and a human mother from whose relation to one another and to oneself may be learned our relation to nature, the universal mother, and to that immortal spirit which is the father of us all. We are given, moreover, the symbol of the tree, which, rooted in the earth, its mother, and nourished by her juices, strives ever upward towards its father, the sun. The mathematician may be able to demonstrate, as a result of a lifetime of hard thinking, that unity and infinity are but two aspects of one thing; this is not clear to ordinary minds, but made concrete in the tree—unity in the trunk, infinity in the foliage—any one is able to understand it. We perceive that all things grow as a tree grows, from unity to multiplicity, from simplicity and strength to beauty and fineness. The generation of the line from the point, the plane from the line, and from the plane, the solid, is a matter, again, which chiefly interests the geometrician, but the inevitable sequence stands revealed in seed, stem, leaf, and fruit: a point, a line, a surface, and a sphere. There is another order of truths, also, which a tree teaches: the renewal of its life each year is a symbol of the reincarnation of the soul, teaching that life is never-ending climax, and that what appears to be cessation is merely a change of state. A tree grows great by being firmly rooted; we too, though children of the air, need the earth, and grow by good deeds, hidden, like the roots of the tree, out of sight; for the tree, rain and sunshine: for the soul, tears and laughter thrill the imprisoned spirit into conscious life.

We love and understand the trees because we have ourselves passed through their evolution, and they survive in us still, for the arterial and nervous systems are trees, the roots of one in the heart, of the other in the brain. Has not our body its trunk, bearing aloft the head, like a flower: a cup to hold the precious juices of the brain? Has not that trunk its tapering limbs which ramify into hands and feet, and these into fingers and toes, after the manner of the twigs and branches of a tree?

Closely related to symbolism is sacramentalism; the man who sees nature as a book of symbols is likely to regard life as a sacrament. Because this is a point of view vitalizing to art let us glance at the sacramental life, divorced from the forms and observances of any specific religion.

This life consists in the habitual perception of an ulterior meaning, a hidden beauty and significance in the objects, acts, and events of every day. Though binding us to a sensuous existence, these nevertheless contain within themselves the power of emancipating us from it: over and above their immediate use, their pleasure or their profit, they have a hidden meaning which contains some healing message for the soul.

A classic example of a sacrament, not alone in the ordinary meaning of the term, but in the special sense above defined, is the Holy Communion of the Christian Church. Its origin is a matter of common knowledge. On the evening of the night in which He was betrayed, Jesus and His disciples were gathered together for the feast of the Passover. Aware of His impending betrayal, and desirous of impressing powerfully upon His chosen followers the nature and purpose of His sacrifice, Jesus ordained a sacrament out of the simple materials of the repast. He took bread and broke it, and gave to each a piece as the symbol of His broken body; and to each He passed a cup of wine, as a symbol of His poured-out blood. In this act, as in the washing of the disciples' feet on the same occasion, He made His ministrations to the needs of men's bodies an allegory of His greater ministration to the needs of their souls.

The sacrament of the Lord's Supper is of such beauty and power that it has persisted even to the present day. It lacks, however, the element of universality—at least by other than Christians its universality would be denied. Let us seek, therefore some all-embracing symbol to illustrate the sacramental view of life.

Perhaps marriage is such a symbol. The public avowal of love between a man and woman, their mutual assumption of the attendant privileges, duties and responsibilities are matters so pregnant with consequences to them and to the race that by all right-thinking people marriage is regarded as a high and holy thing; its sacramental character is felt and acknowledged even by those who would be puzzled to tell the reason why.

The reason is involved in the answer to the question, "Of what is marriage a symbol?" The most obvious answer, and doubtless the best one, is found in the well known and much abused doctrine, common to every religion, of the spiritual marriage between God and the soul. What Christians call *the Mystic Way,* and Buddhists *the Path* comprises those changes in consciousness through which every soul passes on its way to perfection. When the personal life is conceived of as an allegory of this inner, intense, super-mundane life, it assumes a sacramental character. With strange unanimity, followers of the Mystic Way have given the name of marriage to that memorable experience in "the flight of the Alone to the Alone," when the soul, after trials and purgations, enters into indissoluble union with the spirit, that divine, creative principle whereby it is made fruitful for this world. Marriage, then, however dear and close the union, is the symbol of a union dearer and closer, for it is the fair prophecy that on some higher arc of the evolutionary spiral, the soul will meet its immortal lover and be initiated into divine mysteries.

As an example of the power of symbols to induce those changes of consciousness whereby the soul is prepared for this union, it is recorded that an eminent scientist was moved to alter his entire mode of life on reflecting, while in his bath one morning, that though each day he was at such pains to make clean his body, he made no similar purgation of his mind and heart. The idea appealed to him so profoundly that he began to practise the higher cleanliness from that day forth.

If it be true, as has been said, that ordinary life in the world is a training school for a life more real and more sublime, then everything pertaining to life in the world must possess a sacramental character, and possess it inherently, and not merely by imputation. Let us discover, then, if we can, some of the larger meanings latent in little things.

When at the end of a cloudy day the sun bursts forth in splendor and sets red in the west, it is a sign to the weather-wise that the next day will be fair. To the devotee of the sacramental life it holds a richer promise. To him the sun is a symbol of the love of God; the clouds, those worldly preoccupations of his own which hide its face from him. This purely physical phenomenon, therefore, which brings to most men a scarcely noticed augmentation of heat and light, and an indication of fair weather on the morrow, induces in the mystic an ineffable sense of divine immanence and beneficence, and an assurance of their continuance beyond the dark night of the death of the body.

When the sacramentalist goes swimming in the sea he enjoys to the full the attendant physical exhilaration, but a greater joy flows from the thought that he is back with his great Sea-Mother—that feminine principle of which the sea is the perfect symbol, since water brings all things to birth and nurtures them. When at the end of a day he lays aside his clothes—that two-dimensional sheath of the three-dimensional body—it is in full assurance that his body in turn will be abandoned by the inwardly retreating consciousness, and that he will range wherever he wills during the hours of sleep, clothed in his subtle four-dimensional body, related to the physical body as that is related to the clothes it wears.

To every sincere seeker nature reveals her secrets, but since men differ in their curiosities she reveals different things to different men. All are rewarded for their devotion in accordance with their interests and desires, but woman-like, nature reveals herself most fully to him who worships not the fair form of her, but her soul. This favored lover is the mystic; for ever seeking instruction in things spiritual, he perceives in nature an allegory of the soul, and interprets her symbols in terms of the sacramental life.

The brook, pursuing its tortuous and stony pathway in untiring effort to reach its gravitational centre, is a symbol of the Pilgrim's progress, impelled by love to seek God within his heart. The modest daisy by the roadside, and the wanton sunflower in the garden alike seek to image the sun, the god of their worship, a core of seeds and fringe of petals representing their best effort to mimic the flaming disc and far-flung corona of the sun. Man seeks less ardently, and so more ineffectively in his will and imagination to image God. In the reverent study of insect and animal life we gain some hint of what we have been and what we may become—something corresponding to the grub, a burrowing thing; to the caterpillar, a crawling thing; and finally to the butterfly, a radiant winged creature.

After this fashion then does he who has embraced the sacramental life come to perceive in the "sensuous manifold" of nature, that one divine Reality which ever seeks to instruct him in supermundane wisdom, and to woo him to superhuman blessedness and peace. In time, this reading of earth in terms of heaven, becomes a settled habit. Then, in Emerson's phrase, he has hitched his wagon to a star, and changed his grocer's cart into a chariot of the sun.

The reader may perhaps fail to perceive the bearing of this long discussion of symbols and sacraments upon the subject of art and architecture, but in the mind of the author the correlation is plain. There can be no great art without religion: religion begins in consciousness as a mystic experience, it flows thence into symbols and sacraments, and these in turn are precipitated by the artist into ponderable forms of beauty. Unless the artist himself participates in this mystic experience, life's deeper meanings will escape him, and the work of his hands will have no special significance. Until it can be said of every artist

"Himself from God he could not free,"

there will be no art worthy of the name.

SELF-EDUCATION[1]

I take great pleasure in availing myself of this opportunity to speak to you on certain aspects of the art which we practise. I cannot forget, and I hope that you sufficiently remember, that the architectural future of this country lies in the hands of just such men as you. Let me dwell then for a moment on your unique opportunity. Perhaps some of you have taken up architecture as you might have gone into trade, or manufacturing, or any of the useful professions; in that case you have probably already learned discrimination, and now realize that in the cutting of the cake of human occupations you have drawn the piece which contains the ring of gold. The cake is the business and utilitarian side of life, the ring of gold is the æsthetic, the creative side: treasure it, for it is a precious and enduring thing. Think what your work is: to reassemble materials in such fashion that they become instinct with a beauty and eloquent with a meaning which may carry inspiration and delight to generations still unborn. Immortality haunts your threshold, even though your hand may not be strong enough to open to the heavenly visitor.

Though the profession of architecture is a noble one in any country and in any age, it is particularly rich in inspiration and in opportunity here and now, for who can doubt that we are about to enter upon a great building period? We have what Mr. Sullivan calls "the need and the power to build," the spirit of great art alone is lacking, and that is already stirring in the secret hearts of men, and will sooner or later find expression in objective and ponderable forms of new beauty. These it is your privilege to create. May the opportunity find you ready! There is a saying, "To be young, to be in love, to be in Italy!" I would paraphrase it thus: To be young, to be in architecture, to be in America.

It is my purpose tonight to outline a scheme of self-education, which if consistently followed out I am sure will help you, though I am aware that to a certain order of mind it will seem highly mystical and impractical. If it commends itself to your favor I shall be glad.

Many of you will have had the advantage of a thorough technical training in your chosen profession: be grateful for it. Others, like Topsy, "just growed"—or have just failed to grow. For the solace of all such, without wishing to be understood to disparage architectural schooling, I would say that there is a kind of education which is worse than none, for by filling his mind with ready-made ideas it prevents a man from ever learning to think for himself; and there is another kind which teaches him to think, indeed, but according to some arbitrary method, so that his mind becomes a canal instead of a river, flowing in a predetermined and artificial channel, and unreplenished by the hidden springs of the spirit. The best education can do no more than to bring into manifestation that which is inherent; it does this by means of some stimulus from without—from books and masters—but the stimulus may equally come from within: each can develop his own mind, and in the following manner.

The alternation between a state of activity and a state of passivity, which is a law of our physical being, as it is a law of all nature, is characteristic of the action of the mind as well: observation and meditation are the two poles of thought. The tendency of modern life and of our active American temperament is towards a too exclusive functioning of the mind in its outgoing state, and this results in a great cleverness and a great shallowness. It is only in moments of quiet meditation that the great synthetic, fundamental truths reveal themselves. Observe ceaselessly, weigh, judge, criticize—this order of intellectual activity is important and valuable—but the mind must be steadied and strengthened by another and a different process. The power of attention, the ability to concentrate, is the measure of mental efficiency; and this power may be developed by a training exactly analogous to that by which a muscle is developed, for mind and muscle are alike the instruments of the Silent Thinker who sits behind. The mind an instrument of something higher than the mind: here is a truth so fertile that in the language of Oriental imagery, "If you were to tell this to a dry stick, branches would grow, and leaves sprout from it."

There is nothing original in the method of mental development here indicated; it has been known and practised for centuries in the East, where life is less strenuous than it is with us. The method consists in silent meditation every day at stated periods, during which the attempt is made to hold the mind to the contemplation of a single image or idea, bringing the attention back whenever it wanders, killing each irrelevant thought as it arises, as one might kill a rat coming out of a hole. This turning of the mind back on itself is difficult, but I know of nothing that "pays" so well, and I have never found any one who conscientiously practised it who did not confirm this view. The point is, that if a man acquires the ability to concentrate on one thing, he can concentrate on anything; he increases his competence on the mental plane in the same manner that pulling chest-weights increases his competence on the physical. The practice of meditation has moreover an ulterior as well as an immediate advantage, and that is the reason it is practised by the Yogis of India. They believe that by stilling the mind, which is like a lake reflecting the sky, the Higher Self communicates a knowledge of Itself to the lower consciousness. Without the working of this Oversoul in and through us we can never hope to produce an architecture which shall rank with the great architectures of the past, for in Egypt, in Greece, in mediaeval France, as in India, China, and Japan, mysticism made for itself a language more eloquent than any in which the purely rational consciousness of man has ever spoken.

We are apt to overestimate the importance of books and book learning. Think how small a part books have played in the development of architecture; indeed, Palladio and Vignola, with their hard and fast formulæ have done the art more harm than good. It is a fallacy that reading strengthens the mind—it enervates it; reading sometimes stimulates the mind to original thinking, and *this* develops it, but reading itself is a passive exercise, because the thought of the reader is for the time being in abeyance in order that the thought of the writer may enter. Much reading impairs the power to think originally and consecutively. Few of the great creators of the world have had use for books, and if you aspire to be in their class you will avoid the "spawn of the press." The best plan is to read only great books, and having read for five minutes, think about what you have read for ten.

These exercises, faithfully followed out, will make your mind a fit vehicle for the expression of your idea, but the advice I have given is as pertinent to any one who uses his mind as it is to the architect. To what, specifically, should the architectural student devote his attention in order to improve the quality of his work? My own answer would be that he should devote himself to the study of music, of the human figure, and to the study of Nature—"first, last, midst, and without end."

The correlation between music and architecture is no new thought; it is implied in the famous saying that architecture is frozen music. Vitruvius considered a knowledge of music to be a qualification of the architect of his day, and if it was desirable then it is no less so now. There is both a metaphysical reason and a practical one why this is so. Walter Pater, in a famous phrase, declared that all art constantly aspires to the condition of music, by which he meant to imply that there is a certain rhythm and harmony at the root of every art, of which music is the perfect and pure expression; that in music the means and the end are one and the same. This coincides with Schopenhauer's theory about music, that it is the most perfect and unconditioned sensuous presentment known to us of that undying *will-to-live* which constitutes life and the world. Metaphysics aside, the architect ought to hear as much good music as he can, and learn the rudiments of harmony, at least to the extent of knowing the simple numerical ratios which govern the principal consonant intervals within the octave, so that, translating these ratios into intervals of space expressed in terms of length and breadth, height, and width, his work will "aspire to the condition of music."

There is a metaphysical reason, too, as well as a practical one, why an architect should know the human figure. Carlyle says, "There is but one temple in the world, and that is the body of man." If the body is, as he declares, a temple, it is no less true that a temple, or any work of architectural art is in the nature of an ampler body which man has created for his uses, and which he inhabits, just as the individual consciousness builds and inhabits its fleshly stronghold. This may seem a highly mystical idea, but the correlation between the house and its inhabitant, and the body and its consciousness is everywhere close, and is susceptible of infinite elaboration.

Architectural beauty, like human beauty, depends upon a proper subordination of parts to the whole, a harmonious interrelation between these parts, the expressiveness of each of its functions, and when these are many and diverse, their reconcilement one with another. This being so, a study of the human figure with a view to analyzing the sources of its beauty cannot fail to be profitable to the architectural designer. Pursued intelligently, such study will stimulate the mind to a perception of those simple yet subtle laws according to which nature everywhere works, and it will educate the eye in the finest known school of proportion, training it to distinguish minute differences, in the same way that the hearing of good music cultivates the ear.

It is neither necessary nor desirable to make elaborate and carefully shaded drawings from a posed model; an equal number of hours spent in copying and analyzing the plates of a good art anatomy, supplemented with a certain amount of life drawing, done merely with a view to catch the pose, will be found to be a more profitable exercise, for it will make you familiar with the principal and subsidiary proportions of the bodily temple, and give you sufficient data to enable you to indicate a figure in any position with fair accuracy.

I recommend the study of Nature because I believe that such study will assist you to recover that direct and instant perception of beauty, our natural birthright, of which over-sophistication has so bereft us that we no longer know it to be ours by right of inheritance— inheritance from that cosmic matter endowed with motion out of which we are fashioned, proceeding ever rationally and rhythmically to its appointed ends. We are all of us participators in a world of concrete music, geometry and number—a world, that is, so mathematically constituted and co-ordinated that our pigmy bodies, equally with the farthest star, throb to the music of the spheres. The blood flows rhythmically, the heart its metronome; the moving limbs weave patterns; the voice stirs into radiating sound-waves that pool of silence which we call the air.

> "Thou canst not wave thy staff in air,
> Or dip thy paddle in the lake,
> But it carves the bow of beauty there,
> And ripples in rhyme the oar forsake."

The whole of animate creation labours under the beautiful necessity of being beautiful. Everywhere it exhibits a perfect utility subservient to harmonious laws. Nature is the workshop in which are built *beautiful organisms*. This is exactly the aim of the architect—to fashion beautiful organisms; what better school, therefore, could he have in which to learn his trade?

To study Nature it is not necessary to go out into the fields and botanize, nor to attempt to make water colours of picturesque scenery. These things are very well, but not so profitable to your particular purpose as observation directed toward the discovery of the laws which underlie and determine form and structure, such as the tracing of the spiral line, not alone where it is obvious, as in the snail's shell and in the ram's horn, but where it appears obscurely, as in the disposition of leaves or twigs upon a parent stem. Such laws of nature are equally laws of art, for art *is* nature carried to a higher power by reason of its passage through a human consciousness. Thought and emotion tend to crystallize into forms of beauty as inevitably, and according to the same laws, as does the frost on the window pane. Art, in one of its aspects, is the weaving of a pattern, the communication of an order and a method to lines, forms, colors, sounds. All very poetical, and possibly true, you may be saying to yourselves, but what has it to do with architecture, which nowadays, at least, is pre-eminently a practical and utilitarian art whose highest mission is to fulfil definite conditions in an economical and admirable way; whose supreme excellence is fitness, appropriateness, the perfect adaptation of means to ends, and the apt expression of both means and ends? Yes, architecture is all of this, but this is not all of architecture; else the most efficient engineer would be the most admirable architect, which does not happen to be the case. Along with the expression of the concrete and individual must go the expression of the abstract and universal; the two can be combined in a single building in the same way that in every human countenance are combined a racial or temperamental *type*, which is universal, and a *character*, which is individual. The expression of any sort of cosmic truth, of universal harmony and rhythm, is the quality which our architecture most conspicuously lacks. Failing to find the cosmic truth within ourselves, failing to vibrate to the universal harmony and rhythm, our architecture is—well, what it is, for only that which is native to our living spirit can we show forth in the work of our hands.

Your work will be, in the last analysis, what you yourselves are. Let no sophistry blind you to the truth of that. There are rhythms in the world of space which we find only in the architecture of the past, and enamoured of their beauty we repeat them over and over (off the key for the most part), on the principle that all the songs have been sung; or we just make a noise, on the principle that noise is all there is to architecture anyway. It is not so. Those systems of spatial rhythms which we call Egyptian, Classic, Gothic, Renaissance architecture and the rest, are records all of the living human spirit energizing in the stubborn matter of the physical plane with joy, with conviction, with mastery. When that undying spirit awakes again in you, stirred into consciousness by meditation, which is its prayer; by music, which is its praise; by the contemplation of that fair form which is its temple; and by communion with nature, which is its looking-glass; you will experience again that ancient joy, hold again that firm conviction, and exercise again that mastery to transfuse the granite and iron heart of the hills into patterns unlike any that the hand of man has made before.

[Footnote 1: An address delivered before the Boston Architectural Club in April, 1909.]

Note from the Editor

Odin's Library Classics strives to bring you unedited and unabridged works of classical literature. As such, this is the complete and unabridged version of the original English text unless noted. In some instances, obvious typographical errors have been corrected. This is done to preserve the original text as much as possible. The English language has evolved since the writing and some of the words appear in their original form, or at least the most commonly used form at the time. This is done to protect the original intent of the author. If at any time you are unsure of the meaning of a word, please do your research on the etymology of that word. It is important to preserve the history of the English language.

Taylor Anderson

Made in United States
North Haven, CT
25 November 2023

44530175R00039